TRUCKS

THE WORLD'S GREATEST TRUCKS

TRUCKS

THE WORLD'S GREATEST TRUCKS

INGRID PHANEUF AND JAMES MENZIES

p

This is a Parragon Publishing book
First published in 2006

Parragon Publishing
Queen Street House
4 Queen Street
Bath BA1 1HE, UK

ISBN 1-40546-724-X

Editorial and design by
Amber Books Ltd
Bradley's Close
74–77 White Lion Street
London N1 9PF
www.amberbooks.co.uk

Project Editor: Sarah Uttridge
Design: Zoe Mellors
Picture Research: Terry Forshaw

Printed in China

CONTENTS

Introduction

Trucks are unlike cars—not just because they are larger and more powerful but because they exist for different reasons. While cars gained popularity soon after their introduction in the late nineteenth century as glamorous toys for the rich, trucks were of the masses and for the masses. They were ugly, noisy and smelly and the only justification for their existence would be that they made sense. Economic sense.

What do we think about trucks? Why do we have to have them? Most people in the developed world are familiar with cars since they own one but the very same people often regard trucks as a blight on society. Those lumbering "juggernauts" that clog up the highways are a source of frustration. Life, in their view, would be so much better if there weren't any trucks. Whichever view one takes, modern society relies on trucks. It is no exaggeration to say that we could not sustain our way of life without them.

In the century or so since horseless carriages became a reality, trucks have served an increasingly important role in industry and commerce. When the first self-propelled load carriers were invented in the late nineteenth century they were greeted with a mixture of suspicion, fear and even derision. Those early experimental machines were so crude and inefficient that they were not taken seriously. Such contraptions, it was thought, would never rival the horse-drawn wagon.

If one event gave credibility to the potential of motor trucks it was World War I. The rapid movement of troops and munitions revolutionised the way the war was fought. The post-war glut of ex-army trucks kick-started a new era of civilian road

haulage. With that came an ever-growing network of main roads. Ironically, roads that were needed for the long distance transport of goods required trucks to help build them.

Once it became practical to haul heavy loads over long distances, society benefited from a wider choice of products. Supplies of perishable foods such as meat, fish, milk and fruit could be distributed over wider areas. Other important commodities such as fuel—coal, wood and oil—could be transported

Above: *The Western Star LowMax epitomizes what many North American owner/operators look for in a truck – a long, square hood, spacious sleeper cab, and plenty of chrome.*

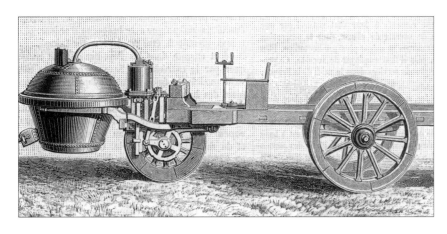

Above: *Cugnot's development of the steam dray was funded by the French King Louis XV.*

Below: *While most drivers were forced to sit out in the open air, the Volvo series 1 trucks could be fitted with a cab on demand. This was probably due to the cold climate in Sweden.*

of "back-yard" truck builders some of whom flourished while others fell by the wayside. Many of the survivors grew into vast concerns, absorbing smaller manufacturers on the way. Trucks became progressively more efficient and capable of carrying heavier loads. Specialised bodywork enabled a wider variety of products to be transported safely and efficiently.

With the increase in road transport came the need for tighter legislation to govern the size, weight and performance of trucks. Such legislation, combined with innovative engineering, shaped the modern truck as we know it. Modern demands for even greater performance and driver comfort, increased safety and reduced emissions, have seen that process of development continue. Depending on their country of origin, today's trucks carry up to 30 tons (30 tonnes) at speeds of 56 mph (90 km/h)—a far cry from the solid-tyred bone-shakers of World War I when five tonnes was considered a big load and 12mph (20 km/h) a good speed!

Love them or loath them, trucks serve a vital role in our lives. Without them our stores, bars and filling stations would be empty. Without them manufacturing industry would grind to a halt as supplies of raw materials dried up. Just about everything we eat, drink, wear and use in our daily lives comes to us by truck.

from the suppliers to the customer quickly and efficiently. True, such movement of goods began with the arrival of inland waterways and railways some half a century earlier but road haulage had the added benefit of a rapid door-to-door service.

During the first two decades of the twentieth century truck manufacturers explored various modes of propulsion including steam, gasoline and electric power. Both steam and electric vehicles had shortcomings in that their unladen weight was higher, limiting the "payload", while the distance they could cover was also limited. The internal combustion engine emerged as the most efficient means of propulsion. That efficiency improved further with the arrival of the diesel engine in the mid-1920s.

In the early days there were large numbers

CUGNOT
⚒ 1769 France

CUGNOT'S STEAM DRAY

Built by French army officer Nicholas Cugnot, the "grandfather" of the modern truck, this steam-powered truck was intended to transport cannons for the French army.

Inset: *Nicholas Cugnot's steam dray could carry up to 5 tons at 2 mph (3.3 kph) but could only generate enough steam to travel about 700 yards (640m) before stopping to build up more steam.*

Left: *With a heavy boiler mounted ahead of its single front wheel Cugnot's vehicle was inherently unstable and is said to have collided with a stone wall while being demonstrated. Consequently its driver was responsible for the first recorded traffic accident.*

The steam dray had three wheels with iron rims, two at the back and one in front. The steam power came from a boiler hooked up to a two-cylinder engine, both of which were mounted over the front wheel of the vehicle. It could travel at 2.48mph (4km/h), stopping every 10 to 15 minutes to build up enough steam pressure to get going again.

In 1771, Cugnot built a second vehicle for testing which was a tractor designed for a 4–5 ton payload. Cugnot sought the approval of France's Minister of War at the time, the Marquis de Monteynard, for some secret tests to be staged at Versailles. Secrecy was necessary at this time because of the fact that Cugnot and some of his highly placed supporters at the court of Louis XV viewed the steam dray as something of a national military secret. Despite this, the tests were never conducted, because the Minister did not give his approval or even answer Cugnot's letters.

First truck accident

Tests were conducted, nevertheless, and the vehicle was soon credited with causing the world's first traffic accident by colliding with a garden wall. In spite of such accidents, one of Cugnot's vehicles survived the French Revolution and today resides in the National Academy of Arts and Sciences in France.

Napoleon took little interest in steam-powered gun tractors, so Cugnot and his steam-powered vehicles sadly faded into obscurity immediately after the Revolution.

Specifications

Country: France

Year manufactured from: 1769

Engine: two cylinder, steam powered

Transmission: not available

Payload: 4 tons (4 tonnes)

Applications: cannonball carrier

Special features: one powered wheel in front

TREVITHICK
1803 UK

LONDON STEAM CARRIAGE

In 1803, Richard Trevithick and his associate Andrew Vivian designed the London Steam Carriage, a coachlike, steam-powered vehicle capable of going up to 9.9mph (16km/h).

Right: *Though built to carry passengers, Trevithick's London Steam Carriage could, in theory, have been adapted to carry up to half a ton of goods. However, it would have been rather top-heavy and, being a tricycle, not too stable.*

James Watt was the first to patent "parallel motion" in steam engines, which could keep a rigid piston rod moving vertically while attached to the end of an oscillating beam. He was also one of the first to use a definite measurement to compare steam-power to horsepower. One horsepower was exactly 33,000 foot-pounds of work per minute. Within a few years, Watt's engines were frequently referred to as 14-horse engines, 20-horse engines, and so on.

The London Carriage

Following on from Watt's ideas, in 1803, Trevithick (who also worked with Watt) and his associate Andrew Vivian assembled the London Carriage at Felton's carriageworks in Leather Lane. On completion, the carriage was driven about 10 miles (16km) through the streets of London with seven or eight passengers, in an attempt to demonstrate to the public that self-powered passenger and/or cargo vehicles were a possibility.

While the experiment was considered successful, the vehicle proved highly unpopular, mainly because it terrified horses, but also because of several deaths due to horrific boiler accidents. There was also the issue of fires caused by sparks from the funnels. The media and public largely ignored the London Carriage and the vehicle was eventually dismantled.

Specifications

Country: UK
Year manufactured from: 1803
Engine: two cylinder, steam powered
Transmission: not available
Payload: not available
Applications: experimental
Special features: first self-powered passenger carrying vehicle in the world

BOLLÉE

⚒ 1873 France

L'OBÉISSANTE

Amédée Bollée was one of the most ingenious French engineers of his time. Despite its old-style design, *L'Obéissante* was a very advanced steam vehicle.

Left: *Frenchman Amédée Bollée did much to advance steam-carriage design with his* l'Obéissante, *which was the first vehicle to feature Ackerman-type steering controlled by a steering wheel.*

Amédée Bollée was born in 1844. His father was a bell founder in the city of Le Mans. At first, the young Amédée worked in the foundry, where he perfected a new casting process. In 1867, he visited the French Exposition Universelle in Paris. There he saw steam carriages, and as an engineer took interest in this vehicle and began to work on a new project. Three years after the 1870 Franco-Prussian war, the steam carriage *l'Obéissante* (the Obedient One) was ready. The vehicle contained real craftsmanship, with accommodation for 12 passengers, a roof, and windows, the overall style being like that of a train passenger car. The quiet steam boiler at the rear was

another masterpiece. It burned 110lb (50kg) of coal per hour and the two cylinders under the floor could move *l'Obéissante* from 9 to 25mph (15 to 40km/h). This amazing top speed (for the time) was offset by a small range of 16 miles (25km). But the most advanced design within the steam carriage was the steering wheel, the first one in the automotive industry.

Disappointment

After trials, *l'Obéissante* proved itself a very capable vehicle, and at the end of 1875 it made Le Mans to Paris (114 miles/183km) in only 18 hours. Bollée, however, was unable to sell the vehicle.

Specifications

Country: France

Year manufactured from: 1873

Engine: steam boiler with two cylinders

Transmission: not available

Payload: up to 12 passengers

Applications: utility steel truck

Special features: first steering wheel, independent front suspension, full forward control

BENZ

⚒ 1885–89 Germany

BENZ MOTOR WAGEN

Unlike steam engines, the internal-combustion engine operates by burning fuel inside the engine. With the introduction of the four-stroke internal-combustion engine from 1885, the era of the true truck begins.

Right: *Carl Benz perfected the first practical internal combustion-engined vehicle—a three-wheeled "motor wagen." It was powered by a horizontal single-cylindered engine which could run on gasoline, paraffin, or naptha.*

Specifications

Country: Germany

Year manufactured from: 1885

Engine: four stroke internal combustion powered by paraffin, gasoline, or napta

Transmission: not available

Payload: not available

Applications: experimental

Special features: three wheels

The forerunner of trucks powered by internal combustion engines was a Benz three-wheeler. It could run on paraffin, gasoline, or naphtha, and could reach 9.3mph (15km/h). Benz's first motorized vehicle eventually featured three innovations still in use in trucks and cars today—an electric battery, spark plug, and electric coil ignition—but not from the very beginning. Benz's first electric ignition used a generator, but the generators of the early 1880s were not up to the task, so the inventor shifted to a storage battery. The vehicle's spark plug consisted of two pieces of insulated platinum wire stuck into the combustion chamber.

No fuel injection
The fuel induction system also left something to be desired. The engine didn't use fuel injection or anything resembling a true carburettor. Instead, fuel drained into a can filled with fabric fibers and then evaporation carried the fumes into the cylinder.

Even so, the vehicle's four-stroke engine worked, the four strokes of the engine consisting of intake, compression, power, and exhaust. And after a major reorganization of the company in 1890, the Benz motor works was on its way to becoming a successful manufacturer of vehicles.

PEUGEOT
1895 France

PEUGEOT TYPE 13

The Peugeot brothers introduced five units of the Type 13, the company's first gasoline-powered truck, in 1895. The truck was a light delivery vehicle, with a Daimler internal-combustion engine.

Specifications

Country: France
Year manufactured from: 1895
Engine: gas powered internal combustion
Transmission: chain drive
Payload: 882lb (400kg)
Applications: light delivery truck
Special features: first commercial vehicle by Peugeot

In 1888, Armand Peugeot's fascination with motorized vehicles was born. He very proudly unveiled a Peugeot steam-powered tricycle at the Paris World Fair. But he also started to experiment with gasoline-powered engines, and produced four units of the first gasoline-powered four-wheel car, called the Type 2, fitted with a Daimler engine at the Valentigney factory.

It would soon include solid rubber or optional Michelin tires with rubber tubes, thanks to Edouard Michelin, who tried out his pneumatic tires on the company's Éclair model car in the Paris–Bordeaux–Paris race of 1895.

Heavy-duty production

By 1900 Peugeot was manufacturing several heavy-duty vehicles (for that time) including the Type 18 eight-seater bus with proprietary Peugeot engine (Armand stopped buying Daimler's engines from Panhard and Levassor in 1896), the Type 22 two-seater pickup truck, and the Type 32 wagonette-tonneau (21 units in 1900). The Type 34 and 35 commercial vehicles quickly followed. The Type 36 single-cylinder was the first tonneau with a hood at the front and a steering wheel with an inclined steering column instead of handlebars. It marked Peugeot's move to chainless transmission.

Above: *France's earliest light delivery truck was based on the Peugeot Type 13 of which five were produced as early as 1895. They were powered by Daimler gasoline engines.*

W.J. STILL
1899 Canada

W.J. STILL ELECTRIC DELIVERY WAGON

Less than a year after Robert Simpson purchased his Fischer No. 2 Coach Delivery Wagon, Parker Dye Works purchased a Toronto-made electric delivery wagon from the W. J. Still Motor Company.

Specifications

Country: Canada

Year manufactured from: 1899

Engine: battery powered electric

Transmission: belt driven, rear-wheel drive

Payload: not available

Applications: delivery

Special features: Ackerman-type steering

Above: Like all electric vehicles the Still was limited to local deliveries because its batteries needed regular recharging. It did, however, boast some advanced features including Ackerman-type steering.

The wagon surely provoked the envy of the driver of the Fischer wagon, because the driver of the Still wagon was provided with lower seating under a protective roof. The motor was midmounted, with a belt driving the rear wheels.

Ackerman steering
The Still wagon was also more stable, thanks to the inclusion of Ackerman-type steering. The Ackerman Steering Principle defined the geometry applied to all vehicles (two- or four-wheel drive) to enable the correct turning angle of the steering wheels to be generated when negotiating a corner or a curve. Before the principle was developed, horse-drawn carriages had parallel steering arms and suffered from poor steering performance (tending especially to tip while cornering at high speeds). Rudolf Ackerman is credited with working out that using angled steering arms would cure these vehicles of such steering problems.

Electric cars and trucks enjoyed popularity both in North America and Europe at the turn of the century.

SAURER
✖ 1903 Switzerland

SAURER FIVE-TONNER

The first Saurer truck was built by Adolph Saurer at his factory in Arbon, Switzerland, in 1903. It grossed 5 tons (5.08 tonnes), and was powered by a four-cylinder, T-head, 25 to 30hp (18.6 to 22.3kw) engine.

The truck proved popular, collecting trophies at several international contests. Factories were erected in Paris and Lindau, Germany, and the company started distributing in Russia, Canada, and Japan. The trucks first appeared in the U.S. in 1911. By then Saurer trucks ranged from 1.5 to 3.5 tons (1.52 to 3.55 tonnes), all of them with four-cylinder engines producing 16 to 30hp (11.9 to 22.3kw) and four-speed transmissions. The smaller trucks were shaft-driven, while the larger ones used chains.

The trucks were so successful in Europe that by 1914, Saurer was producing 130 different models. The company's success continued into World War I, when the company's Paris factory produced military trucks. (They were converted for use as postal trucks after the war.) Throughout that period, many Saurer trucks continued to use wooden wheels, even though the general industry trend was toward solid rubber. Engines came in 321.7, 412.7, and 491.6ci (5.3-, 6.8-, and 8.1-liter) sizes, with outputs of 42, 52, and 62hp (31.3, 38.7, and 46.2kw).

From solid to pneumatic tires
By the end of the 1920s Saurer trucks had finally made the transition to solid rubber and then pneumatic tires, and many trucks

Above: *The 1903 Saurer 5-tonner was unusual for a heavy truck of that period in featuring shaft drive. Soon after production commenced, however, this was changed to chain drive.*

were using diesel. In diesel use, at any rate, Saurer was a leader. It would be 10 years before other truck manufacturers began to use diesel extensively.

The 1930s saw the birth of the C-line series, which ranged in weight from 1 to 6 tons (1.016 to 6.09 tonnes). Smaller models contained four-cylinder, 169.9ci (2.8-liter), 50hp (37.2kw) diesel engines, or six-cylinder, 176ci (2.9-liter), 52hp (38.7kw) gasoline engines. When fuel supplies were scarce during World War II, the trucks came with wood-gas generators as well.

A product of World War II, and one of Saurer's most impressive achievements, was the heavy-duty M4H, used for transporting ammunition. The tractor was forward control (meaning the driver sat ahead of the front axle and by definition the engine) with four-wheel drive and a four-cylinder, 70hp (52.1kw) engine with a 1.5-ton (1.52-tonne) capacity. By the standards of the day, it was extremely powerful.

Below: The 1930s saw the birth of the C-line series, which included one- to six-tonners.

Specifications

Country: Switzerland	**Payload:** up to 2.5 tons (2.54 tonnes)
Year manufactured from: 1903	**Applications:** delivery, military
Engine: four cylinder gasoline powered	**Special features:** T-head engine
Transmission: shaft or chain driven, four-speed	

AUTOCAR
✗ 1908 USA

AUTOCAR XVII

The original Autocar company began as the Pittsburgh Motor Car Company, founded in 1897 by brothers Louis and John Clark. Two years later, they moved the company to Pennsylvania, and renamed it Autocar.

The company began focusing on trucks in 1907, with the introduction of the Autocar Model XVII—a two-cylinder 2-ton (2.03- tonne) truck with shaft-driven axle. By 1911, the company had switched over to making trucks exclusively.

The Autocar truck chassis quickly earned the reputation of lending itself to almost every style of body, a foreshadowing of the truck's forthcoming use in multiple applications. In 1925, Autocar advertised in the *National Petroleum News* that "More even weight distribution on all four wheels is an added Autocar advantage for hauling shifting loads of gasoline and oil." In 1926, the company introduced the Autocar Model 26,

a four-cylinder 5-ton (5.08-tonne) vehicle. A six-cylinder, cab-forward design was introduced in 1930.

First diesel engines

In 1935, the first diesel engines, supplied by Kenosha, were introduced. By 1940 Autocar offerings included heavy trucks with a variety of tractions, including 6x2s, 6x4s, 6x6s, and even 8x4s.

Autocar was the first truck manufacturer to build wheels with wooden instead of wire spokes, and is credited by automotive historians with several other truckmaking firsts. It was the first company to mass produce a truck with forward control (a

Above: *Early Autocar trucks were of 2 tons (2.03 tonnes) payload capacity and of forward-control layout, which the company claimed provided more even weight distribution and greater load space within the overall length.*

configuration in which more than half the engine length is behind the farthest-front point of the windshield base and the steering wheel hub is in the first quarter of the vehicle length). It offered the first four-cylinder-engine forward-control truck. And it was one of the few truck manufacturers to make its own engines, transmissions, and rear axles. In addition, some historians cite Autocar trucks as being instrumental in the Allied forces' victories in both World Wars.

Advertisements appeal to patriotism

A print advertisement published in 1943 cashed in on the patriotic sentiment aroused by the Autocar at that time:

"TANKERS AWEIGH ! Massive, six-wheel tank trucks...for the Navy...Bristling Half Tracks for the Army...Rugged mobility for the Marine Corps and the Air Forces.... All essential. All for Uncle Sam. All training the men and women of Autocar to build the sturdy, dependable Autocar Truck that the world will need when war is won. So keep your pledge to the U. S. Truck Conservation Corps. Your trucks are your own, but their life belongs to the Nation."

Autocar obtained U.S. government authorization for heavy-duty hauling in 1945, a fact the company did not hesitate to boast of in print advertisements:

"HEAVY TANKAGE! For the ruts of War or the highway of Peace, Autocar Trucks are precision-built for the heaviest of heavy-duty work. Mile after mile, day after day, year after year, these famous trucks put on dependable, low-cost-per-mile performance and reduced hauling and delivery costs for the nation's leaders. Ask Shell Union Oil Corporation. They know Autocar Trucks through long years of rugged use.... Follow the leaders, for they know the way," reads an advertisement printed in 1945.

White buys controlling interest

The White Motor Car Co. purchased a controlling interest in Autocar in 1953, and White was purchased by Volvo in 1981. In 1988, Volvo GM Heavy Truck Corp. was formed as a joint venture between Volvo and General Motors Corp. At the time, Volvo GM's nameplates were WHITE GMC and Autocar. The WHITE GMC nameplate was discontinued in 1995 and Volvo GM's trucks were sold under the Volvo and Autocar nameplates, the latter continuing to appear on heavy-duty construction trucks.

In July 2001, Grand Vehicle Works Holding Corporation (GVW) announced the purchase of the AutoCar Class 8 Xpeditor truck line from Volvo. Called LCF trucks (Low Cab Forward) the trucks were used primarily used in the vocational market. Autocar celebrated its 100th birthday in 1997.

Specifications

Country:	USA
Year manufactured from:	1908
Engine:	two cylinder gasoline powered
Transmission:	three-speed
Payload:	two tons (2.03 tonnes)
Applications:	multiple, body customized for buyer
Special features:	Chassis lent itself to almost every style of body

Left: *After 1919 Autocar moved up the weight range with models capable of carrying 3 tons (3.04 tonnes), 4 tons (4 tonnes), and 5-ton (5.08-tonne) payloads. Forward control was the norm until 1926 when conventional trucks were added to the range.*

RENAULT
1910 France

RENAULT TRUCK

The 1910 Renault was built for versatility. It was used for a variety of applications, including delivery and general urban transportation. The Renault story started in 1898, when Louis Renault founded the company.

By 1900, production rose to 179 cars and by 1903, Renault had built its first heavy-duty (for the time) chassis for commercial use. The chassis earned the company a contract for supplying Paris taxis and was partially responsible for production climbing to 1,200 units in 1905. In 1907, Renault had produced a bus, and introduced it in 10- and 15-seater versions at the Ninth Paris Motor Show.

As was the case with many early 1900s truckmakers, Renault owed a great deal of its success as a heavy-duty chassis manufacturer to the war. By 1917, Renault was producing the "Diamond brand" design—the first modern tank. The company produced 30 of these tanks per day at its plant in Vernisseaux.

Award winners

By the mid-1920s, Renault tractors and 7-ton (7.1- tonne) trucks were garnering awards. The company was the first to offer a road tractor fitted with a Servo vacuum assisted brake. Renault also manufactured trucks powered by gas generators to promote the use of fuels other than gasoline.

The scheme seems to have succeeded because by the 1930s Renault was producing diesel-powered trucks. Unfortunately the Nazi occupation of France in World War II temporarily tarred the company's reputation—its trucks were extensively used by Germany.

After the war, Louis Renault was found guilty of collaboration and as a result, the company was confiscated and nationalized.

Above: *This 1909 model has a sloping hood which was a characteristic of all early Renaults.*

Specifications

Country: France

Year manufactured from: 1910

Engine: gasoline powered

Transmission: not available

Payload: not available

Applications: multiple, chassis also used for taxis and busses

Special features: built for versatility

FEDERAL

1910 USA

FEDERAL TRUCK

In its newsprint advertisements, the Federal Motor Truck Company of Detroit, Michigan, proclaimed itself the "largest manufacturer of 4½ and 3½ ton (4.57 and 3.55 tonne) worm drive motor trucks exclusively".

Right: *What originated as the Bailey Motor Truck Co became the Federal Motor Truck Co and the first chain drive 1-tonner of 1910 was based on a Bailey prototype. Power came from a 4-cylinder gasoline engine.*

Specifications

Country: USA

Year manufactured from: 1910

Engine: gasoline powered

Transmission: belt drive

Payload: one ton (1.016 tonne)

Applications: haulage, agricultural, delivery, municipal

Special features: by 1920s Federal trucks were being exported overseas

At that time, Federal mainly manufactured trucks that could carry a 1-ton (1.016-tonne) payload. The 1910 design was highly conventional, and looked very much like a car, with its radiator and gasoline engine in the front and its driver sitting behind it under a metal awning.

It had spoked steel wheels with solid rubber tires, and the chassis had two frames rails, which appear to be as close together as a car's. (The wheels, however, were set out from the frame rails, making it easier for them to fit into the ruts that were typical of many American roads at that time.) The truck could reach speeds of up to 20mph (32km/h).

Ford an early convert

Henry Ford, of the Ford Motor Company, would buy the very first model, fitted out with a wood-slat box on top of a flatbed, for use on his farm. This vehicle survives in the Henry Ford Museum in Dearborn, Michigan, to this day. Ford was one of the truck's earliest converts (commercial motor vehicles were, at that time, still competing with horse-drawn carriages). In fact, many motor-truck advertisements of the time pointed out how motorized transportation was a more cost-effective haulage method than horse-drawn carriages. Federal was not alone in trying to convince the potential truck buyers of this.

MACK
1916 USA

MACK AC "BULLDOG"

The Mack AC truck was introduced in 1916. With its chain-drive rear axle, the truck soon earned a reputation for reliability and durability. It saw continued success, remaining in production for 24 years.

Above: *The Mack AC "Bulldog" had a formidable reputation for toughness. British soldiers in World War I were so impressed by its tenacity that they nicknamed it "Bulldog." Mack subsequently adopted the quintessentially British breed as its company emblem.*

Even before World War I, Mack had established a good international reputation. The company had already built many British military trucks, as well as an armored car on an AB chassis for the New York National Guard.

Chief engineer Edward Hewitt was credited with designing Mack's AC model, which had 18 patents to cover all of its innovations. The truck's radiator was placed behind its engine, and air was drawn from the hood, forced through the radiator, and then sent through screening at the front. This unique design was believed to prevent the damage to exposed radiators that was apparently being caused, accidentally or not, by antitruck lobbyists. (It was led by U.S. trade unionists who feared, justifiably as it turns out, that motorized vehicles would put horse-drawn transportation out of business.)

Another innovation was the positioning of the steering wheel at a 45-degree angle, which would prove to be considerably more comfortable for the driver. As for the engine, it was rated at 74bhp (55.18kw). (The acronym "hp" stands for "Brake Horsepower" and refers to the actual or useful horsepower of an engine, usually determined from the

force exerted on a friction brake or dynamometer connected to the drive shaft.) The press chrome-nickel steel frame rails were heat-treated for durability, as were the pair-cast cylinders. Lightweight aluminum was used for the radiator tank, the transfer case, the timing cover, and the engine crankcase. The front axle was made of dropforged alloy steel to make the AC tougher.

Selective transmission

The AC had a selective three-speed transmission and a clutch brake. It also had an all-steel cab with an optional metal roof—a substantial improvement on the more common exposed wooden seats of the day. The design proved extremely popular. During World War I, Mack delivered approximately 4500 AC model trucks of 3.5-ton (3.55-tonne), 5.5-ton (5.58-tonne), and 7.5-ton (7.62-tonne) capacity for the government of the United States, which had adopted the truck as a standard military vehicle. These went overseas to France with American doughboys.

Mack also produced and delivered more than 2,000 units to Great Britain during the same period. British soldiers reportedly referred to Macks as "bulldogs," calling out "Aye, send in the Mack Bulldogs!" when faced with a difficult transportation problem. British mechanics and soldiers apparently believed the trucks had the tenacity of a bulldog. As the bulldog was the symbol of Great Britain at that time, this was high praise indeed. The Americans needless to say, shared the opinion of the British, at least according to company historians. Of course, the nickname could also easily have been due to the appearance of the trucks, with their snub noses. Whatever the case, the nickname stuck. AC and Mack trucks in general would eventually became widely known as "the Bulldog Macks," and by 1922 the company adopted the Bulldog as its corporate symbol.

Bulldog ornament

As for bulldog hood ornament, it wouldn't come along until much later. First, a picture of a bulldog (first drawn in 1921) would appear on a sheet-metal plate riveted to each side of the cab, showing the bulldog chewing up a book entitled "Hauling Costs," with the name "Mack" on his collar and "International Motor Company" underneath. (The name of the company, which had been changed to International Motor Company after a merger with two other truckmakers, would be changed back to Mack in 1922 to prevent the company from being confused with another US truckmaker, the International Harvester Company.)

Left: In frontal appearance the Mack AC, with its radiator-behind engine layout, bore an uncanny resemblance to the French Renault. Ironically Mack was eventually absorbed into Renault Véhicules Industriels in 1990.

Below: Even before World War I, Mack had established an international reputation.

Specifications

Country: USA	**Payload:** one to seven and a half tons (1.016 to 7.63 tonnes)
Year manufactured from: 1916	
Engine: gasoline powered	**Applications:** delivery, military
Transmission: three-speed selective with clutch brake	**Special features:** radiator behind engine

FORD TT
⚒ **1917 USA**

FORD TT ONE-TONNER

Henry Ford built his first experimental commercial vehicle—a panel truck—in 1899. But it wasn't until 1917 that the Ford Motor Company brought out the TT one-tonner—basically a beefed-up Model T car.

A machinist's apprentice at the tender age of 16 in 1863, Ford's engineering skills had become evident from an early age. He soon became chief engineer for the Edison Illuminating Company in Detroit, Michigan. By 1903 Ford and a group of investors, who believed in his genius, had founded the Ford Motor Company.

First Ford truck
The first commercial vehicle produced by the company was the Model E delivery wagon (a later version of the panel truck mentioned above). It proved useful for city deliveries and Ford Motors would continue to manufacture it through 1911. By then Ford had become known mainly for manufacturing light trucks and cars. Most famous of all, of course, was Ford's Model T car, otherwise known as the "Tin Lizzy."

But Henry Ford soon gained renown as an industrialist as well. He became the first automotive manufacturer (and the first North American manufacturer) to introduce

Above: Henry Ford's legendary Model T was joined by a heavier model, the TT 1-tonner, in 1917. The simple rugged low-cost workhorse took the truck market by storm.

assembly-line production to his factory. He was also the originator of salaries of $5 per day for workers (which was considered a good wage at that time) as well as the creator of the 40-hour working week.

Ford would continue to develop trucks. The Model TT truck, produced in 1917, was Ford's first venture into the big-rig market. With its solid rubber tires, wood-spoked wheels, and canvas tarpaulin, the first Model TT wasn't much to look at. But later versions, with carved wood-paneled bodies, solid roofs, electric lights, pneumatic tires, and glass windshields, would substantially improve the TT's overall looks and saleability. The first TT was powered by a 177ci (2898cc) engine (positioned over the front axle and in front of the driver, "conventional" style) with three-speed transmission. The truck chassis, though modeled on the Model T, had a longer and sturdier frame. The wheelbase was also 2ft (61cm) longer and the Model TT had a stiffer rear suspension than the Model T did.

Ford creates modern assembly line

As he'd done with his other vehicles, Ford immediately put his assembly-line magic to work for the Ford Model TT. No fewer than 25 Model TT truck chassis rolled off the production line each day. By 1922, the number of trucks produced by Ford per day had grown to 193,294 units, a testimony to Ford's ability to survive the war's end, thanks to the fact the company continued to produce civilian vehicles throughout the war. In short, while the war in Europe had ultimately meant the end of companies that had overinvested in wartime truck production, it had only helped increase Ford's truck sales abroad and at home.

The Depression years that followed had their effect, with Ford truck sales falling just like everyone else's. Still, because of Ford's light-truck business and the affordability of its vehicles, its sales remained healthier than most. What finally brought full recovery to the company was Ford's introduction of the Flathead (also known as an L-head) V-8 engine in 1932. The engine would be offered in all the company's truck models as well as its cars.

Introduction of V-8

Ford engineers cut corners by casting the engine in a single piece rather than several. By doing so they also reduced the number of engine parts, which increased durability (but also made it harder to repair). The end result was that the V-8 engine boosted Ford truck and car sales and reestablished the company as the industry leader.

Inset: *Simplicity was the keynote of Ford's design, exemplified by its single transverse front spring. The TT was inexpensive to buy and inexpensive to maintain.*

Specifications

Country:	USA
Year manufactured from:	1917
Engine:	gasoline powered
Transmission:	three-speed, chain driven
Payload:	one ton (1.016 tonne)
Applications:	delivery
Special features:	later versions included electric lights, pneumatic tires, etc.

Below: *One of the TT's strengths was its adaptability to a host of different special duties, such as this dump truck for small consignments of building materials.*

LIBERTY
⚒ **1918   USA**

LIBERTY CLASS B

The Liberty Class B was designed by a committee of American military officials, members of the American Society of Automotive Engineers, and volunteers from 45 American manufacturers.

The Liberty concept was born, like most other inventions, out of necessity. The Allied forces in Europe were having a hard time maintaining and repairing their trucks during World War I. U.S. military officials soon realized that military trucks made of standardized and interchangeable parts would improve their situation considerably.

Standard design
Specs for the standard Liberty Class B, 4x2, 3-ton (3.04-tonne) truck were submitted to U.S. Army officials in July 1917, and a design committee was formed. By October 1917, two prototype trucks had been built and were available for testing. (The engine block

was made by Continental, its cylinder heads by Waukesha, and its pistons by Hercules.) The trials proved so successful that by mid-November, the U.S. government had already signed contracts for the manufacture of the Liberty B's standardized components.

The final Standard B 5-ton (5.08-tonne) would be 21ft 9in (6.6m) long by 7ft (2.1m) wide and 6ft 3in (1.9m) high. It would have four forward and one reverse gear, a 160.5-in (4.07-m) wheelbase, and front tires that were smaller than the rear ones. The truck's L-head engine would measure 425ci (255cc) and run four cycles, with 52bhp (38.7kw). Production of the Standard B Liberty truck would begin in April 1918.

Above: *The need to standardize military trucks to simplify spare-part supplies and maintenance led to the Liberty, which was built by a number of U.S. manufacturers starting in 1918.*

Specifications

Country: USA

Year manufactured from: 1918

Engine: gasoline powered

Transmission: four-speed transmission, low gear reduction

Payload: three tons (3.04 tonnes)

Applications: military

Special features: produced by multiple manufacturers for military

PIERCE ARROW TRUCK

1920 USA

PIERCE ARROW

Pierce Arrow trucks built nearly 7,000 of its cab-behind-engine trucks for export in 1918 alone. Their original truck had been a cab-over-engine design, but it didn't do well during testing so was abandoned.

Above: *Pierce Arrow of Buffalo, New York, were one of the earliest truck builders to introduce worm-drive axles when most other heavy trucks featured chain drive.*

Specifications

Country: USA
Year manufactured from: 1920
Engine: dual valve gasoline powered
Transmission: worm drive
Payload: not available
Applications: multiple
Special features: dual ignition, shockproof windshield glass and backup lights

The massive demand for Pierce Arrows overseas would make it one of the most respected truckmakers in North America at that time, ranked alongside Packard and Alco in terms of quality and expense. The period following the war was bad for truckmakers in that demand was way down, but good in that the U.S. government had finally realized the importance of building roads.

The United States Army had made its first transcontinental road trip from Washington, D.C., to San Francisco in 1919, in part to encourage the Government to invest in a national interstate road system for defense purposes. Dwight D. Eisenhower, a Captain in the Army at that time, went along for the ride. After 62 days of treacherous travel on dirt roads and crumbling bridges, Eisenhower and his contemporaries were convinced that better roads were the answer. The government would subsequently shell out $75 million on building roads and making improvements.

Fifth wheel standardized

Truck manufacturers were ready with improvements of their own. The fifth wheel was patented and became standardized on trucks in 1920. Backup lights were standard by 1922, and shockproof glass was used in windshields by 1926. But Pierce Arrow was ahead of the pack as usual, as their 1920 truck already had all of these features. It also had dual ignition and a dual-valved engine for more power and better fuel economy. And it could also be hooked up to different trailers.

HUG

1922 USA

HUG MODEL T

In 1921, Hug decided to build its own trucks to suit its business specifications. Rugged but reliable, the Hug truck range was used during the twenties and the thirties for the big American construction projects.

Left: *The Hug Model T was a "no frills" machine built along simple rugged lines and aimed at the construction industry.*

With its open cab and its simple design, the Model T was a rugged truck designed for heavy applications. It was fitted with a Buda 34hp (25kW) gasoline engine and a Warner three-speed transmission with a Clark spiral bevel axle, as well as two-wheel brakes. The top speed was about 45mph (72km/h), double the speed of many other trucks from the same period. The rubber tires, with dual rear tires, were uncommon for a severe-duty truck and despite a small size the Model T could carry a load of up 2 tons (2.03 tonnes). It was bodied with a dump or with a concrete mixer. In the middle of the twenties, three other models were built, with payloads from 1½ tons to 3½ tons (1.52 to 3.56 tonnes). Like all the Hug trucks until 1932, they were powered by Buda engines. Hug used subcontractor-built components like Clark, Columbia, Timken, or Wisconsin axles and Brown-Lipe or Fuller transmissions. These trucks kept the rugged, "no-frills" appearance, and in 1927 a massive six-tonner with a seven-speed gearbox appeared. After 1930, the range was completed with the "Roadbuilder" series and, for the first time, the series was available with Caterpillar diesel engines. At the beginning of the war, Hug manufactured some 6x6 military trucks, but no contracts were concluded and 1942 was the last production year for the company.

Specifications

Country: USA
Year manufactured from: 1922
Engine: four cylinder Buda engine, 34hp (25kw)
Transmission: three-speed
Payload: two tons (2.03 tonnes)
Applications: dump truck, concrete mixer
Special features: rubber tires, open cab

CHENARD AND WALCKER
✖ **Mid 1920s France**

CHENARD & WALCKER

For most people, Chenard & Walcker was a car manufacturer. However, it was also an innovative truck builder. In France, its contribution to the semitrailer combination was significant.

Above: The Chenard & Walcker UT was one of the first tractors ever built.

Specifications

Country: France	
Year manufactured from: 1927	
Engine: four cylinder gasoline powered 20hp (15kW)	
Transmission: three-speed	
Payload: 1.96 to 9.84 tons (two to ten tonnes)	
Applications: semitrailer or trailer hauling	
Special features: short wheelbase truck, trailer coupling system	

The prestigious Chenard & Walcker company was founded in France in 1901 and was famous for its cars. In 1920, the company was the fourth-largest car manufacturer in the country.

FAR company

At the end of the World War I, the company created a new department, the FAR company, in order to exploit the patented Lagache et Glazsmann trailer-coupling system. Their trailers and semitrailers initially had a very limited distribution, and it was not until the sixties that they spread throughout Europe. Chenard & Walcker wanted to prove that a small short-wheelbase tractor could haul more payload than a rigid truck on short distances. The tractor could haul a trailer to a warehouse, uncouple the trailer while it was unloaded, and return to base for a further haul. This system was more profitable than using a rigid truck. The company built two- or three-axle bonneted tractors. Some heavy 6x4 axle configurations, with chain drive, were designed for logging applications or special big haulages. Some of them were sold as omnibus tractor units in Holland.

INTERNATIONAL HARVESTER

✕ **1928 USA**

INTERNATIONAL HARVESTER SIX-SPEED SPECIAL

By 1928, the International Harvester Company (IHC) of America had already established a name for its trucks, and not just back in rural America, but also for multiple applications in cities.

International Harvester trucks were being sold in countries as far away as Japan, where IHC chassis were marketed for multiple applications, including commercial hauling, municipal work and passenger transportation. Commercial haulers were available in sizes from 3,000 to 10,000lb (1,360.5 to 4,535kg) payload capacity, with Speed Truck light- to medium-duty vehicles in 1¼-, 1½-, 2-, and 3-ton (1.27-, 1.52-, 2.03,

and 3.04-tonne) versions and heavy-duty trucks in 2½-, 3½-, and 5-ton (2.54-, 3.55-, and 5.08-tonne) models. They could be fitted with express bodies, panel bodies, dump bodies with an under-body hoist, and special bodies for any purpose. For municipal work, they could be fitted as fire trucks, garbage trucks, ambulances, police wagons, street maintenance vehicles, etc. For passenger transportation the sky was the limit.

Above: *Launched in 1928, International's "Six Speed Special" one-tonner featured a two-speed rear axle, which, combined with the normal three-speed gearbox, provided six forward and two reverse ratios.*

Six-speeder returns to roots

The International Harvester Six-Speed Special truck, introduced in 1928, was the company's first truck with a two-speed rear axle (for going in reverse—the truck also had six speeds going forward.) It was specially designed for off-road rural haulage and became popular immediately. (In fact, earlier versions of the Six-Speed Special had already contributed to doubling International Harvester truck sales in the last three years.)

The Six-Speed Special owed at least some of its popularity to the fact that it was a return to the company's farming roots (IHC had started out producing one of North American's first motorized reapers.) But the Six-Speed Special double reverse wasn't the sole contributor to the company's success.

Marketing goldmine

In 1928, IHC management hit on an idea that would become a tried-and-true truck-marketing goldmine thereafter. In the age of America's love affair with the romance of the desert (Howard Carter had discovered Tutankhamun's tomb in 1922) why not promote a truck used by someone who had conquered it? The idea soon paid off, in the form of an article/advertisement in the pages of the October 1928 edition of *Scientific American.*

The article, with the hero/explorer in the foreground and an International half-ton panel truck in the back, told the story of Sir Charles Markham and Baron Frederick Von Blixen-Fineke's 3,000-mile (4,828km) trek through the Sahara desert in the world's first four-wheel truck to do so. The truck had a fully covered cab and body, with unglazed windows on all sides to allow the desert air to circulate more freely (though as one would expect there was a system for covering the windows in case of sandstorms). It had an engine in front, and remountable pneumatic tires (as well as several spares fastened to the body) and appeared to have been tough enough to endure the extreme temperatures and sand of the world's biggest desert.

The article describes in detail a first-person account of the journey made by Sir Charles, but of course it does not go so far as to give any details as to whether the truck suffered from any unforeseen mechanical problems on the journey or not.

Specifications

Country:	USA
Year manufactured from:	1928
Engine:	gasoline powered
Transmission:	six-speeds forward, two speeds reverse
Payload:	up to 5.08 tonnes (five tons)
Applications:	multiple
Special features:	specially designed for off road haulage

Left: *With its roots in the agricultural industry, International Harvester produced tough trucks that were highly popular among farmers who often needed to traverse unmade roads.*

INTERNATIONAL
SIX-SPEED
SPECIAL

The 2-Speed Axle

The Only
Speed Truck Built with
Two Complete Power Ranges

REO SPEED WAGON
1929 USA

REO SPEED WAGON STANDARD 1½-TONNER

The REO Speed Wagon was named after its designer, Ransom Eli Olds (1864–1950), who founded the Olds Motor Vehicle Company in Lansing, Michigan, in 1897 and later the REO Motor Company.

Above: *Reo first adopted the "Speed Wagon" name for its trucks in 1915 and progressively updated the range through to 1939 when the last Speed Wagons were built. This is a late 1930s two/three-tonner with a tipping body.*

One of his most popular vehicles, the REO Speed Wagon (from which a popular rock group of the 1970s later took its name) was originally fitted out as flatbed pickup truck. It was very high speed and heavy duty and was considered a milestone of transportation history. Its rugged ability to withstand the rough roads of North America in the early 1900s meant it would eventually be developed to service multiple applications. Over the years it would see service as a tow truck, fire truck, fuel delivery truck, in short, for all applications that required a rugged workhorse design.

Indeed, advertisements for the truck in the 1920s boasted, "This REO Speed Wagon fits every business... Even in those lines where you would naturally think only in terms of 10-ton trucks, we find Speed Wagons rendering splendid—and owners tell—more economical...."

REOs (cars included) were popular all the way up to the time of the Great Depression, and were reportedly capable of logging 100,000 miles (160,930km) without abnormal wear and tear. Fans claim the

Speed Wagon set the standard that most companies producing trucks at that time tried to imitate.

The first REO Speed Wagon was a ¾-tonner. It was advertised as being capable of up to 22mph (35.4km/h)—although those who used it claimed it could reach 40mph (64.3km/h)—even when fully loaded. The Speed Wagon had an electric starter and a 45hp (33.5kw), four-cylinder engine. It also had a 13-plate clutch and three-speed selective sliding gear transmission, and bevel drive.

Several models available

By the end of the "Roaring Twenties" the Speed Wagon chassis was available in several models, including the Junior ½-ton, the Tonner, the Standard 1½-ton with two choices of wheelbase, the Master (2 tons), and the Heavy Duty (3 tons).

The 1929 Speed Wagon had a six-cylinder engine, with L-type head, 3.25in (8.2cm) bore, and 4in (10.1cm) stroke. It had four-point suspension, seven-bearing crankshaft, and aluminum-alloy pistons. It also had a thermostatic temperature control, semi-automatic spark control, and a single-plate clutch. As was usual at that time, the chassis could be customized with a coupe cab (or not) and there were three standard body styles available (full panel, stake (wood panel flatbed) or Express, available with or without a canopy top.) The vehicle rode on spoked, malleable iron artillery wheels and pneumatic tires, with a suspension that included extra-long semi-elliptical springs. Speed Wagons of the time also had four wheel internal hydraulic brakes, a standard 23in (58cm) wheelbase, and an irreversible steering gear, not to mention an automatic chassis oiling system.

But more than that, Olds' Speed Wagon trucks were popular for their stylish designs, as well, not to mention the backing of the familiar Olds name. At its height in the 1920s, the factory in Lansing, Michigan employed about 6,000 people.

Customer testimonials

By 1930, testimonials alone would sell the trucks: "It might interest you to know that my second two-ton REO Speed Wagon has passed the 65,000-mile mark with a repair expense of but $201.10, and I expect to run it another 66,000 miles," reads a customer testimonial published in 1930. REO stopped making cars altogether in 1936 and changed hands several times starting in the 1950s, eventually merging with the Diamond T division of the Cleveland-based White Motor Company.

Specifications

Country: USA

Year manufactured from: 1929

Engine: four cylinder

Transmission: three-speed selective sliding

Payload: ¾ ton (0.76 tonnes)

Applications: delivery

Special features: electric starter

Below: *The Speed Wagon was ruggedly built from the beginning and boasted powerful performance. A variety of body types for different applications was available.*

DELAHAYE
1929 France

DELAHAYE PS 92

Delayahe was one of Europe's most advanced car manufacturers at the beginning of the 20th century. The company was founded in Tours, but quickly re-established itself in Paris under Emile Delahaye.

The company was famous for fire engines and fire apparatus. Hence the major part of Delayahe's income was the truck business, especially during World War I. Delahaye became renowned for its beautiful engines: all the Delayahe engines were fast and powerful—exactly what a fire truck needed when a rapid response was required.

PS 92

After World War I, Delayahe brought the fire engine and fire truck ranges up to date. The best example of this modernization is the PS 92. The Premier Secours Model 92 ("First Aid" fire truck) was very popular in all French rural districts until the fifties. This fire engine was smaller than previous models, but had an improved practicality. In many ways it was a thoroughly modern fire truck, with a pump driven by the engine (called "Petit cheval", i.e. "Little Horse"), a 3182-liter (700-gallon) water supply, an independent hose reel and a six-man crew. It had a 30kw (40hp) four-cylinder engine, but the radiator size was increased to avoid overheating when the pump was being operated.

Above: *The Delahaye PS 92 was one of the early fire trucks produced in France.*

Specifications

Country: France

Year manufactured from: 1929

Engine: four cylinders overhead valves engine, 30 kw (40hp)

Transmission: not available

Payload: not applicable

Applications: fire engine

Special features: engine driven pump

BERLIET
1930   France

BERLIET DIESEL-POWERED TRUCK

Marius Berliet started experimenting with automobiles in 1894. His first car was built in a shed. Because he had to be able to get it out through the garden gate, it could only be as wide as that.

Above: *Berliet introduced its first diesel engines in 1930. They were of the indirect injection type.*

Specifications

Country:	France
Year manufactured from:	1930
Engine:	diesel powered Martin
Transmission:	chain drive
Payload:	not available
Applications:	ideal for long haul
Special features:	France's first diesel-powered truck

Berliet produced his first truck, for a silk manufacturer, in 1897. The first trucks were built on car chassis, but they mounted some of the biggest engines of the time—as much as 80hp (59.6kw). They were also forward control. Berliet eventually received the ultimate recognition as a truckmaker, producing 40 CBA trucks per day for the French military during the battle of Verdun in 1916. In 1917, both Berliet and Renault produced a tank specifically ordered by the French government, known as "the Diamond brand." During the war, Berliet

produced up to 16 of these tanks every day at its plant in Venisseux.

Introduction of diesel-powered trucks

Berliet introduced France's first diesel-powered truck in 1930. It had a Martin diesel engine (Martin was a French manufacturer that had produced its first diesel engine in 1928). The new engine certainly stimulated sales because diesel was much less expensive and easier to maintain than gasoline. It also proved more powerful—ideal for the long-distance transportation of goods.

BEDFORD
1930s UK

BEDFORD "W" SERIES

In Bedford nomenclature the first letter indicates model. Some historians of British trucks say a "W" means a chassis made to wartime specifications, although the "W" series reportedly came out in the early 1930s.

Bedford was a subsidiary company of Vauxhall Motors, which was a well known provider of commercial vehicles for the United Kingdom and export markets. It began as the Vauxhall Iron Works, founded by Alexander Wilson in 1857. The company originally built machinery, such as pumps and engines, for the marine industry. It was named Vauxhall because it was first located on Wandsworth Road, in Vauxhall, London.

By the turn of the century Wilson had left the business and the remaining board directors became interested in starting production of a "horseless carriage." The company had already started producing a gasoline-powered launch (one of the first in marine engineering). In 1903, the company was manufacturing a 5hp (3.7kw) single-cylinder car, available to the public for 130 guineas.

Above: The English company Vauxhall Motors started producing the Bedford brand of trucks in the early 1930s. The first trucks of the "W" series were four-wheelers.

The vehicle sold well, and the board of directors decided to expand the production of gasoline-powered vehicles. But in order to do so, the factory would have to move out of London. The company acquired a site in Luton, in Bedfordshire, where it moved in 1905. The company continued to do business under the name Vauxhall Iron Works until 1907, when the modern name of Vauxhall Motors Ltd. and the company's griffin logo was adopted.

Car production continued. Then, in November 1925 Vauxhall was acquired by General Motors. Chevrolet trucks had been on sale in Britain since 1923, but were costly owing to import tax. In 1925 GM set up an operation in Hendon, in Middlesex, to prepare imported vehicles and introduced Buick, Cadillac, Chevrolet, La Salle, Marquette, Oakland, Oldsmobile, and Pontiac cars, as well as Chevrolet and GMC trucks.

But with the country in the grip of a worldwide Depression, there was no little public hostility to imported products. (More than two million people were unemployed in the United Kingdom alone at this time.) So General Motors decided to camouflage its foreign roots by building a completely "British" truck using Vauxhall's Luton plant.

The British truck is born

By the early 1930s, assembly of the last Chevrolet and GMC trucks and vans in Britain had ended and the manufacture of Bedford trucks had begun. In 1930, the first true Bedford was on the road.

The first trucks of the "W" series were four-wheelers—a 30cwt truck and a 2-ton (2.03-tonne) version. The trucks were probably equipped with Bedford's own four- or six-cylinder gasoline-powered engines, which could produce up to 27hp (20.1kw).

The earliest "W" model trucks most probably had four-speed gearboxes attached to bevel drives on the rear axles. It is also safe to assume they had Dewandre servo brakes because those would also appear on the company's commercial passenger vehicles at that time. The trucks proved so successful that by 1937 sales of the Bedford "W" series had reached 30,000.

"W" series on hold

Historians report the "W" series was put on hold during World War II, when the production of civilian and commercial vehicles in Britain was suspended in favor of focusing the nation's efforts on the manufacture of military vehicles. Bedford trucks manufactured during World War II included the "MW" and "OY" types, with modified tractors. Bedford also produced the "QL" 4x4 for military use. After World War II, commercial and civilian production resumed, and Bedford resurrected many of the elements of the original "W" series.

Specifications

Country: UK	
Year manufactured from: 1931	
Engine: four or six cylinder gas powered	
Transmission: four-speed, bevel axle	
Payload: up to 2.03 tonnes (two tons)	
Applications: delivery, military	
Special features: servo brakes	

Below: *Built in Luton, in England, by Vauxhall Motors, Bedford trucks dominated the UK medium-truck market in the 1930s. Vauxhall Motors went on to be a major supplier of military trucks during World War II.*

GMC
1930s USA

GMC HEAVY-DUTY TRUCKS

By the early 1930s, GMC trucks were available with payload capacities of up to 15 tons (13.6 tonnes). Unlike their colleagues at Chevrolet, GMC engineers were focusing on designing heavy-duty trucks.

Specifications

Country: USA

Year manufactured from: 1930s

Engine: six cylinder, gasoline powered

Transmission: five speed, over- and underdrive

Payload: up to 15 tons (15.2 tonnes)

Applications: multiple

Special features: first sleeper-cab optional

Tandem rear axles were already available on trucks like the 10-tonner T0-956 prior to 1933. And by 1933, GMC had fitted its first sleeper cab on a heavy-duty truck, showing the company had a pretty good sense of where trucking was going in terms of long haul. The same year saw downdraft carburettors as well as overhead valve engines adopted in the company's 2-tonner series.

By that time, GMC's heavy-duty trucks were coming standard with 707ci (11.6-liter) six-cylinder engines rated at 173hp (12.9kw). The engine used twin-plate clutches and had a five-speed transmission, with both over- and underdrive. Chain drive or worm drive was the standard on the tandem axles. And for the heaviest trucks, air brakes made by Westinghouse were standard

as well. A six-cylinder, 70hp (52.2kw) side-valve engine, or the larger 120hp (89.5kw) overhead-valve six-cylinder engine were available for trucks with a payload capacity greater than 1.5 tons (1.52 tonnes) in 1934.

Streamlined design

The company redesigned their cabs in 1935, making even the heaviest-duty truck cabs more streamlined. Hydraulic brakes were also added, with full air actuation for the heaviest trucks and hydrovac for medium duty. By 1937, the company had 12 conventional models and 11 cab-over-engine models in its heavy-duty truck line. Diesel engines were standard for the 2- to 6-ton (2.03-to 6.1- tonne) range by 1939, unlike similar models built by Chevrolet.

Above: *GMC heavy trucks of the early 1930s were of very staid appearance but starting in 1936 the company adopted a more streamlined approach with stylish radiator grilles and sloping "vee'd" windshields.*

GENERAL MOTORS
1936 Germany

OPEL BLITZ

General Motors acquired the German motor company Opel AG in 1929. The Opel Blitz was the result of this venture, but with the rise of the Third Reich, the German government decided to nationalize the company.

Specifications

Country: Germany

Year manufactured from: 1936

Engine: four cylinder gasoline 68hp (50kw)

Transmission: not available

Payload: 2.95 tons (three tonnes)

Applications: general-purpose military truck

Special features: 4x2 "S" Type, 4x4 "A" Type, Half Track "Maultier" Type

Above: *Just as General Motors acquired Vauxhall in the UK so it did Opel in Germany. During World War II Opel Blitz military trucks were widely used by the German army.*

More than 100,000 Opel Blitz ("Lightning") were built during World War II. The figure is far from the 800,000 GMC 6x6, but the Blitz was at first planned as a civilian commercial truck. This light vehicle was born in 1931 with a 220-cu.in (3.6-liter) Buick engine (Buick was part of General Motors). The first series had a 1.72-ton (1.75-tonne) payload, which then increased to 2.46 tons (2.5 tonnes) and finally 2.95 tons (3 tonnes) with the most famous Blitz, known as the "S" type. This model made its initial test in 1936 and looked modern with its steel cabin. The gasoline engine was far superior to any of its diesel competitors. After several testings, the Blitz was chosen by the German army. It could accept more than the mentioned payload and its ability to go where no other truck with two-wheel could go is legendary.

Variants

In 1940, Opel built a second version, a 4x4 truck known as the "A" type. About 25,000 of this cross-country Blitz were made and another half-track model was derived from the original frame, codenamed "Maultier" ("Mule"). Only 4,000 entered production, starting in 1942, and most were sent to the Russian front. The Blitz could be customized with various bodies, such as ambulances, tankers, radio-trucks, and general-purpose.

VOLVO
✖ **1931 Sweden**

VOLVO LV66

With the LV 66, the Swedish Volvo company definitively entered the truck market. This truck was indeed a completely new commercial vehicle, designed to compete with the other local truck builder, Scania-Vabis.

Until the beginning of the thirties, Volvo used some car parts in the construction of their trucks. As they began considering increasing the payload of their vehicles, however, the Volvo managers Assar Gabrielsson and Gustaf Larson decided to launch a larger truck with heavy components.

Power problems

From its first appearance on a drawing board, the new truck had to choose between a six- inline or an eight-inline cylinder engine with overhead or flathead valves. Finally, a six inline overhead valves engine was chosen. The gasoline-powered DC 75 engine offered 75hp (56kw) and ran in combination with a new four-speed gearbox. The new LV 66 and 68 ranges were sold from 1931. Different wheelbases and two- or three-axle configurations (from 1933) were available. For the first time, Volvo was also able to sell with a single or a double reduction. In 1933, these ranges could be powered by a new engine, the "Hesselman" engine, based on the gasoline engine, but which could run on diesel fuel thanks to a mechanical injection system. The LV 66 and 68 series were quite popular, and produced reasonable sales figures, but as three-axle trucks or as heavy-duty vehicles, the Volvo DC 75 engine wasn't powerful enough.

Above: The LV66 took Volvo into a heavier weight class in 1931.

Specifications

Country: Sweden

Year manufactured from: 1931

Engine: six cylinder gasoline powered 56kw (75hp)

Transmission: not available

Payload: 3.4 tons (3.5 tonnes)

Applications: delivery truck, tanker, dump truck

Special features: first real Volvo truck, new engine DC 75, new gearbox, and new axle configuration

KENWORTH
mid 1930s   USA

KENWORTH 516 "BUBBLENOSE"

Kenworth unveiled its first cab-over-engine design, the "Bubblenose," in 1936. The truck was designed with a shortened nose to provide maximum payload while complying with the overall state truck length limits.

Above: *Length limits imposed in some states during 1935 led to an increase in cab-over-engine trucks. Typical of the era was the Kenworth 516 "Bubblenose" 6-wheel truck seen here with a drawbar trailer.*

Specifications

Country: USA

Year manufactured from: 1930s

Engine: four or six cylinder gas powered, four cylinder diesel powered

Transmission: five-speed

Payload: up to four tons (3.6 tonnes)

Applications: multiple

Special features: chrome grille

Weight restrictions had also been imposed by the Motor Carrier Act in 1935, so Kenworth had also begun building its own cabs from sheet metal. Chrome was also an esthetic element in the overall Kenworth design; the trucks were instantly recognizable thanks to their chrome grille.

Kenworth partner Harry Kent would not live to enjoy the new design's success. In 1937, he died of a heart attack. Nevertheless, Kent's legacy of cost-cutting and manufacturing efficiencies would continue, resulting in Kenworth becoming increasingly successful over the next three years.

Ten truck models

Among them would be 10 models of trucks, including the 2-ton (2.03 tonne) Model 88, powered by an 83hp (61.9kw) Hercules JXC

engine and the 7-tonner Model 241C powered by a 125hp (93.2k) six-cylinder Cummins diesel engine. Buda and Herschell-Spillman gasoline engines were also available for the 4-tonner model 146B, and the 7-tonner Model 241A. (All gasoline engines had six cylinders by 1937.) The 505, 506, and 507 models were powered by Cummins four-cylinder diesel engines.

Kenworth also got into bus production at the end of the 1930s. The company custom-built the canvas-topped Tri-Coach bus, which could carry 18 passengers, for the Rainier National Park Company. Five of them were delivered to Rainier in 1938. Small buses were also produced. But truck production would continue to be Kenworth's focus, with at least 17 six-wheeled truck models available by 1940.

ERF
1937 UK

ERF OE4

The ERF OE4 weighed only 3 tons (2.72 tonnes) unloaded, but was capable of hauling a 6-ton (5.4-tonne) payload. Like most commercial vehicles of its size built in the UK then, it had a frame swept up over the rear axle.

Specifications

Country: UK

Year manufactured from: 1937

Engine: four cylinder diesel powered Gardner

Transmission: five-speed

Payload: six tons (6.1 tonnes)

Applications: multiple

Special features: could haul twice its weight unloaded

The OE4 had other distinctive design elements as well, thanks to the ingenuity of its designer Ernest Sherratt. The stylish grille was positioned in front of the radiator so as to conceal it. This look was very modern for its time and it would be used for many future ERF trucks in years to come.

The Gardner diesel engine would be used to power the small but powerful OE4. In the late 1930s, Gardner would introduce its 230.6ci (3.8-liter) four-cylinder 4LK diesel engine, capable of up to 57hp (42.5kw) at 2100rpm. The light power unit, with matching transmission, was ideal for the ERF OE4.

By the beginning of 1939, an estimated 40 ERF trucks were rolling off of the production line every month. But six months later, World War II would have its effect on industrial production in the UK.

Design innovation continues

The company did, nevertheless introduce a few new vehicles at the start of the war, including its 7.5-ton (6.8-tonne) dump truck. Engineer Ernest Sherratt designed the truck with two goals in mind: weight reduction and low body-floor height. Weight was strictly controlled by careful selection and integration of parts.

Above: The OE4 was ERF's lightest truck and was powered by a Gardner 4LK diesel which boasted excellent fuel economy.

FODEN
1937   UK

FODEN DG RANGE

It would take time to convince Foden's conservative board members that diesel power would overtake steamers. Several company officials were believers, among them E.R. Foden, his son Dennis, and brother William.

Above: *In 1937 Foden brought out its DG range, powered by Gardner LW series diesel engines with four, five, or six cylinders.*

Specifications

Country: UK

Year manufactured from: 1937

Engine: diesel powered, four to six cylinder Gardner

Transmission: five-speed

Payload: variable

Applications: delivery, then heavy duty

Special features: first Foden diesel trucks

Eventually, E.R. Foden was forced to resign. To Foden's eternal regret, E.R. founded ERF and in June 1933 brought out the diesel-powered C-14, which made the nascent company an almost instant success.

ERF's success and the fact that insurers were increasingly reluctant to insure steam boilers, finally convinced Foden board members that the internal-combustion engine was in fact necessary to the survival of company's commercial vehicle line. Thanks to some of the company's more forward thinkers, Foden had already begun experimenting with gasoline-driven vehicles. Foden then used several gasoline

engines before focusing on diesel trucks such as the R and S-types.

DG range

Finally the company convinced William Foden to come back from Australia. His return heralded the production of the company's first diesel trucks and turned their fortunes around. In 1937 Foden brought out its DG range, powered by Gardner LW series diesel engines with four, five, or six cylinders and with a bore capacity of 84.9ci (1.4 liters). Foden first used these engines in trucks, but their use in heavy-duty commercial vehicles such as ballasted drawbar tractors followed.

FWD
✖ 1937 USA

FWD COEs

According to some truck historians, FWD was the first North American truck manufacturer to introduce the cab-over-engine design to its commercial vehicle range.

Left: In 1937, FWD brought out a COE cab with a two-piece V-shaped windshield. It would be followed by the four-door COE crew cab. Soon COEs would be available in a wide variety of shapes and sizes, even on 6x4s.

The company had its start in 1910, when Otto Zachow, a machinist in Clintonville, Wisconsin, patented a double-Y universal joint in a ball and socket. Zachow's U-joint allowed for the wheels of a vehicle to rotate and be steered simultaneously. With the help of his brother-in-law William Besserdich, who was also a machinist, Otto subsequently built a steam-powered passenger car, which used the new U-joints on its axles.

The steamer wasn't much of a success, so the brothers-in-law turned their hands to gasoline-driven vehicles. Their very first, nicknamed the Battleship, weighed 3,800lb (1,723.3kg). But the brothers still had no intention of getting into automotive manufacture. They just used the vehicle to demonstrate their U-joints. Finally, a group of investors managed to encourage the brothers-in-law to start their own company building four-wheel-drive vehicles. The Four Wheel Drive Automotive Company (FWD) was founded in 1909.

FWD dominates military production

World War I proved profitable for FWD, with the American military ordering so many FWD trucks that other manufacturers were given special licenses to build them as well. Postwar, with half the market flooded with FWD trucks, the company would get by selling spare parts for their maintenance.

Through the 1920s the company made several improvements to its truck line, including introducing pneumatic tires as standard equipment on trucks like the Model B, which had been produced since 1918. The company also focused on building special-purpose trucks, for fire services, utilities, oil hauling, etc.

By the mid-1930s, FWD had innovated further—expanding its product range in terms of payload capacity and powerplants. In 1937, FWD brought out a COE cab with a two-piece V-shaped windshield. It would be followed by the four-door COE crew cab. Soon COEs would be available in a wide variety of shapes and sizes.

Further innovations

FWD introduced new Cummins diesel powerplants as well as double-reduction or multiple-geared axles. With a short wheelbase and a shorter frame than a conventional truck, the COE series could maximize the payload capacity with a longer body or a longer trailer. But the drawback of such a cabin was the engine inside the driver's less roomy cab. The noise, the heat, and the burned-oil smell were uncomfortable, especially during the summer. FWD trucks retained the old-style front cabin during the thirties and didn't keep up with the "streamlined" fashions. The trucks were mainly used in severe-application duties, and the aerodynamic design was secondary. During World War II, FMW supplied the U.S. forces with military trucks. The SU heavy model was built as a COE or Conventional model for the U.S. Marine Corps, and for the Red Army and British forces for use as an artillery tractor. It was powered by a 115hp (86kw) Waukesha gasoline engine and could carry up to 5/6 tons (5.08/6.1 tonnes).

Postwar cabs

After the war, the company used a new cabin built by International, then a Dodge cab was fitted on the new Tractioneer series introduced in 1958. The company also developed custom-designed trucks to utilize Seagrave fire apparatus.

Specifications

Country: USA
Year manufactured from: 1937
Engine: variable
Transmission: five-speed and worm drive
Payload: variable
Applications: multiple
Special features: two piece V-shaped windshield

Left: *FWD Sucoe all-wheel-drive trucks came into their own as military vehicles in World War II.*

FORD
1930s USA

FORD V-8 MODEL BB

In 1932, the new Ford V-8 caused a sensation because it was reliable, smooth, and powerful and had a low-cost flathead engine. It powered the new "BB" type commercial truck chassis that superseded the "AA" types.

The "Flathead" Ford V-8 engine immediately became a success, despite initial casting troubles and overheating problems. With a cast-in-one piece, it had a 90 degree arrangement with a 221-ci (3.6-liter) displacement for 65hp (48kw). It wasn't really sophisticated, but Ford could offer eight cylinders for a price that no other manufacturer could. The new BB-type truck was offered in 131½in (334cm) and 157in (398cm) wheelbase with a new heftier steel frame. The semielliptic springs, an underseat fuel tank, and a revised shaft drive were fitted too. Despite the revolutionary engine, the

Great Depression didn't help sales and Ford had to face up to million-dollar losses. But the fleet operators were very enthusiastic about the V-8 trucks, with their "V-8" logos proudly fixed to the front grille, and in 1934 the engine was improved with a new counterbalanced cast-alloy steel crankshaft, which contributed to increased smoothness by reducing vibrations. A new dual-downdraft Stromberg carburettor was fitted too at this time. In 1935, a new body shell was launched and the revised frame changed the name of the truck series. The "BB" type was phased out to become the Model 51.

Above: *There's no doubt about the engine with the "V-8" logo on the grille clearly displayed.*

Specifications

Country: USA

Year manufactured from: 1932

Engine: eight V cylinders, gasoline powered, 65hp (48kw)

Transmission: three gears

Payload: 1.52 tons (1.5 tonnes)

Applications: stake body, delivery truck, tanker, platform, dump truck

Special features: new V-8 engine

AUSTIN
✠ 1939 UK

AUSTIN K2

In 1939 the Birmingham-based Austin company entered the truck field with an extended range up to a 5-ton (5.08-tonne) payload capacity. The K2 was the most widely used truck.

Above: Austin's new K range of light to medium trucks was first announced in 1939 but full production did not begin until after World War II.

Right: Such was the K model's similarity to its rival, the Luton-built Bedford, that it was nicknamed the "Birmingham Bedford."

Specifications

Country: UK

Year manufactured from: 1939

Engine: six cylinder gasoline

Transmission: four-speeds to bevel

Payload: two tons (2.03 tonnes)

Applications: stake body, parcel delivery truck, dropside platform

The design of the Austin trucks was very similar to the Bedford trucks, and Austin was actually nicknamed the "Birmingham Bedford company." The 2-ton (2.03-tonne) K2 was designed before World War II, but the civilian steel cab model didn't get underway until 1945. During the war, however, about 13,000 K2/Y were built as military ambulances in Austin's Longbridge works.

Postwar service

After the war, the K2 began a new career as delivery van, cattle truck, or dropside wooden platform vehicle. The engine was a well proven gasoline six-cylinder rated at 27hp (20kw) with a four-speed gearbox. The Austin K2 and the bigger 5-ton (5.08-tonne) K4 were very popular on the British roads and they looked modern with a steel roof and a V-windshield. In 1947, a new commercial vehicle entered the range. It was the Three Way Van K8 light truck, which became famous with its forward-control cab and its steel body. At the beginning of 1950, all the conventional K series had a facelift, with more modern hoods and fenders. But they were phased out when Austin merged with the British Motor Corporation in 1951.

SCAMMELL
⚒ **1939–1940 UK**

SCAMMELL PIONEER MILITARY SERIES

The first Scammell articulated truck was a 7.5-tonner built in 1921. From then on the company would focus mainly on building articulated and straight trucks with eight wheels.

In 1927, however, Scammell would come out with the Pioneer, a six-wheeled, off-road heavy-duty tractor with a rocking-type front axle and two feet of vertical movement at each rear wheel. The innovation made for incredible cross-country performance, which would make the Pioneer ideal for use in oil field and lumber operations.

With the outbreak of World War II, the Pioneer would also prove exceptionally useful for the British Army. The truck was used first as a tank transporter, but it would soon be put to other uses as well. The wartime Scammells were equipped with Gardner six-cylinder diesel engines, which gave them the high torque at low speeds they needed for tank and truck recovery operations. And they were also ideal for towing the heavy pneumatic-tired guns used at that time.

Winch or crane

To move guns across ground or to recover stuck vehicles, the pioneer artillery tractor was fitted with a chassis winch in 1939, which could lift 8 tons (8.1 tonnes). The first 43 "breakdown" tractors, designated SV1S or SV1T, were also fitted with folding cranes.

Above: *The Scammell Pioneer's great strength was its exceptional off-road capability.*

Specifications

Country: UK	
Year manufactured from: 1939	
Engine: six cylinder Gardner diesel	
Transmission: five-speed	
Payload: not available	
Applications: heavy duty, off-road, military	
Special features: "breakdown" tractors fitted with folding cranes	

PETERBILT
✕ 1939 USA

PETERBILT 260GD

Peterbilt owed its beginnings to the California-based Fageol Truck Company, a truckmaker that specialized in building trucks for the market in the western United States.

Above: *Peterbilt adapted existing Fageol designs but achieved huge weight savings with extensive use of aluminum alloys.*

Specifications

Country: USA

Year manufactured from: 1939

Engine: diesel powered

Transmission: Cummins four-speed main and three auxiliary, double reduction at rear

Payload: not available

Applications: multiple

Special features: air brakes

Unfortunately, the Depression years would interfere with sales and Fageol would go into receivership in 1932. That was when T.A. Peterman, a lumberman from Washington, started worrying about where he could get good trucks. Peterman had been rebuilding surplus army trucks and modifying old logging trucks for use in his business. But by 1938, his lumber operations had expanded and he needed more trucks. He bought the old Fageol factory and started building custom chain-drive logging trucks in 1939. Of course, it would take some time for Peterman to truly reconcile the ins and outs of truckmaking.

Experiments with aluminum
For instance, the 1939 Model 260GD had an aluminum grille, which reduced weight but

which also broke easily. So the use of aluminum in the grille would be abandoned after just one year.

The engine proved more successful, however. It was an HB6 Cummins diesel that could develop up to 150hp (111.8kw), with a four-speed Brown-Lipe main transmission, as well as a three-speed auxiliary one. The 260GD also came equipped with a Timken double-reduction rear axle and air brakes.

As with most truckmakers, Peterbilt's success or failure would depend largely on road development, industry, and military needs during World War II. While Henry Ford was cranking out hundreds of trucks a day, Peterman set his sights on building 100 trucks a year, concentrating on quality, not quantity. Peterman succeeded building 14 units in 1939 and 82 in 1940.

FREIGHTLINER
⚒ **1940s USA**

FREIGHTLINER CF100 COE

Freightliner trucks appear to be unique in early truck history in that they saw their beginnings in the hauling industry, rather than in engine or bicycle manufacturing.

Leyland James founded Consolidated Freightlines, a hauling company and the forerunner of Freightliner, in 1929 in Portland, Oregon. In true trucker tradition, James was always looking for ways to increase profit and payload. His appetite for finding new ways to do this, particularly when it came to technological innovation, was what led to the creation of Freightliner's very first trucks.

As usual, necessity was the mother of invention. When Leyland James wanted lighter trucks that could carry more payload

and stay within the 60-ft (18.3-m) length limit required by most western U.S. states, the suppliers he dealt with ignored him.

Innovations in materials and design

So, with the help of mechanics already in his employ, James started adapting trucks himself. By the mid-1930s, James and his mechanics had already fitted some of his trucks with lighter aluminum parts, including brake shoes, suspension hanger brackets, and trailer pulleys. Of course, aluminum truck and trailer bodies were the

Above: Being in the trucking business, Leyland James of Consolidated Freightlines knew exactly what kind of truck was required so he and his team went ahead and created the first Freightliner, the CF100.

next logical step. Next came cab-over-engine designs, because by making the tractor shorter, James could increase the length of the trailer, thus increasing payload.

The very first Freightliner cab-over-engine design to hit the road for Consolidated Freightlines was assembled from spare parts and cabs welded together by Freightlines mechanics themselves. It was pulled together from a Fageol truck with a Truck and Coach Company chassis and a custom-designed Freightliner aluminum cab. It had a Cummins diesel engine, and it was a full ton lighter than any other design with a comparable payload.

James' cab-over-engine design proved so successful that the company would build 20 more over the next three years alone. Obviously, James' idea of making trucks lighter and trailers both lighter and longer was working.

Expansion through the 1940s

By 1940, James had finally convinced other carriers, if not manufacturers, of the benefits of lighter, shorter truck designs to increase profits and payload. Consolidated Freightways (James had renamed the company) and five other western carriers

formed the Freightways Manufacturing Company in 1940, to build trucks for their own fleets. The company's first manufacturing plant was opened in Salt Lake City.

James' lightweight COE design was the first truck to be produced. By this time, it had been improved on even more with a heat-treated steel alloy frame and nose for durability. Of course, the aluminum cab and trailer body would be its most distinctive and profitable feature.

But even after opening the Salt Lake City factory, James wasn't really planning to get into the manufacturing business on a permanent basis. He just wanted to build enough trucks to supply himself and the other carriers he'd gone into business with. That all changed when the Freightways Manufacturing Company decided to try to outsource the assembly of its trucks. James and his partners were quickly convinced that the products assembled outside their own plant were vastly inferior to those they'd assembled themselves. That was how Freightways stepped into the manufacturing business permanently, and how what was to become the Freightliner brand of truck was eventually born.

Specifications

Country:	USA
Year manufactured from:	1940s
Engine:	Cummins diesel powered
Transmission:	five or 10-speed
Payload:	not available
Applications:	long haul
Special features:	use of aluminum in parts, bodies, and cabs

Below: *James Leyland convinced five other western American carriers to form the Freightways Manufacturing Company in 1940, to build trucks for their own fleets.*

ALBION
1940s UK

ALBION 6x4 THREE-TON REPAIR TRUCK (MODEL FT103N)

Toward the end of World War II, many British Army trucks were in pretty poor shape. Many of them had been designed before or at the beginning of the war, and had been overhauled several times since.

The army needed a truck on the front line that could repair existing vehicles and carry spares to those who needed them. Because of a dearth of commercially available trucks, they decided to make a limited purchase of Albion 3-tonner commercial trucks as a temporary measure.

Off-road use

The Albion trucks purchased had simple commercial chassis, with six wheels and four-wheel drive. They did not have off-road suspension, but as far as the British Army was concerned, they fitted the bill.

The repair trucks carried a lathe, pillar drills, bench grinders, gas-welding equipment, battery charges, and assorted equipment. The standard Albion Clansman commercial vehicle cabs were used. The bodies had canvas tops and wooden sides, which could be folded down to provide ground-level workbenches. Canvas shelters could even be attached to the sides of the vehicle to provide more workspace on the ground. The FT repair truck was 20ft 9in (6.32m) long, 7ft 6in (2.28m) wide, and 11ft (3.35m) high with an 11ft 9in (3.58m) wheelbase.

Above: *The Albion FT103N repair truck was an adaptation of a 6x4 civilian model.*

Specifications

Country: UK

Year manufactured from: 1940s

Engine: four cylinder diesel

Transmission: chain or worm drive

Payload: three tons (3.04 tonnes)

Applications: military

Special features: sides of bodies could be folded down to provide work benches

PACIFIC CAR AND FOUNDRY
1942   USA

PACIFIC CAR AND FOUNDRY M26 COE

Today PACCAR is best known for having sold various heavy-duty trucks under various famous brand names, including Kenworth, Peterbilt, DAF, Leyland, and Foden.

Specifications

Country: USA
Year manufactured from: 1942
Engine: diesel powered
Transmission: four-speed forward transmission with three speed central transfer case
Payload: 12 tons (12.2 tonnes)
Applications: military tank hauling
Special features: three axles

Above: *The Pacific Car and Foundry Company of Renton, Washington, were responsible for building the U.S. Army's most powerful tractor, the Pacific M26, used to haul tank transporters.*

Pacific Car and Foundry wouldn't build a truck until 1942, when it was commissioned to do so for wartime use by the American armed forces. The U.S. Army needed a vehicle that would be powerful enough to haul tanks loaded onto semitrailers. And Pacific Car and Foundry would deliver just that, when the M26 rolled off its production line.

The M26 would be one of the most powerful trucks built during the war. It was a 6x6, in a cab-over-engine truck-tractor design that could pull 12 tons (12.2 tonnes). It had three axles and a Hall-Scott diesel engine that could develop 240hp (178.9kw). It used a four-speed transmission with a three-speed central transfer case that connected to the rear eight-wheel tandem drive as well as the front two-wheel steering axle (by shaft).

Made for tank and trailer recovery

The truck also had a winch mounted at the front and controlled from the cab and capable of pulling 35,000lb (15,876kg), so it could recover any tractor or trailer lodged in rough terrain. Two more winches were mounted at the rear of the cab.

GMC
1940s   USA

GMC CCKW SERIES AND OTHER WARTIME TRUCKS

The GMC CCKW series of military trucks were made between 1941 and 1945, specifically for the U.S. military during World War II. No fewer than 600,000 Model 353s and 25,000 Model 352s were built in just four years.

They came in several different shapes and sizes, for example, the CCKW-353 had a 13ft 8in (4.1m) wheelbase and was a 6x6, while the CCKW-352 was a 6x4 with a 12ft 1in (3.7m) wheelbase. Both trucks weighed about 5,512lb (2,500kg). Both trucks had six-cylinder overhead-valve diesel engines that could develop up to 90hp (67.1kw) and a maximum speed of 44.7mph (72km/h). The 353 and the 352 both had five-speed overdrive-style gearboxes with two-speed transfer cases, and could go about

about 16 miles to the gallon (400km on 182 liters of fuel). Both trucks were available with hard or soft cabs, and with or without winches. But the U.S. wasn't the only country producing GMC trucks.

Germany takes over
When World War II began in Europe, Germany nationalized the GMC Opel Division. The plant immediately started producing trucks for the Axis powers. By then GM had been established in Europe for

Above: If one truck stuck in the minds of World War II veterans it was the ubiquitous "Jimmy" 2.5-ton (2.54-tonne) 6x6. The GMC CCKW and its 6x4 sister the CCW were built in vast numbers.

some time. In 1923, GM's first European assembly plant was opened in Copenhagen under the name General Motors International A/S. It was to build Chevrolets for sale in Scandinavian countries, the Baltics, Germany, Poland, Czechoslovakia, Austria, Hungary, and Russia. The first GM vehicle to come off the Copenhagen assembly line at the beginning of 1924 was also the first GM to be built outside North America—it was a Chevrolet utility truck. GM went on to establish operations in Antwerp, in Belgium, in 1924.

Vauxhall Motors Ltd., in Luton, England, was acquired by General Motors in 1925. The same year saw General Motors Export Division open its first warehouse in Malaga, Spain, as well as a sales office in Paris and a warehouse in Le Havre, France. Also in 1925, GM opened a sales office in Berlin.

The year 1927 would also see a GM assembly plant built in Berlin. By 1929, GM had acquired Adam Opel AG, based in Rüsselsheim, Germany. Opel would be taken over by the German government in 1940. You might say GM took the war personally.

Dedicated to the war effort

The company converted 100 percent of its production to the war effort as of 1942. During World War II, GM delivered more than $12,300,000,000 worth of war material to lead the Allied war effort, including aircraft engines, aircraft parts, trucks, tanks, marine diesels, guns, shells, and miscellaneous products.

In 1942 alone, the company would produce 148,111 power units solely for military use, which amounted to 16.9 percent of the total truck production in the U.S. that year. By 1943, the company would produce no fewer than 16 different trucks for the U.S. Army. They included 1½- to 3-ton small-arms repair trucks, 1½-ton radio transceiver trucks, 1½- to 3-ton air-compressor trucks, 2½-ton 6x6 artillery tractors, 2½-ton 900-gallon (3,400-liter) tankers, 1½- to 3-ton machine-shop trucks, 2½-ton cargo and troop transporters, 2½-ton cavalry haulers, 1½- to 3-ton earth-boring trucks, 1½-ton recruiting trailer trucks, 2½-ton searchlight carriers, 8-ton arsenal tractor trailers, COE navy fuel tankers, 4-ton anti-aircraft defense trucks, and 1½-ton 4x4 troop transporters.

GMC also produced an estimated 560,000 2½-ton 6x6 trucks for general use. But perhaps the most distinctive vehicle built by GMC during World War II was the amphibious DUKW, know as the "Duck." The vehicle looked like a boat with six wheels (duals in back) and a soft top. It was designed to carry up to 50 men on either land or water.

Inset: It was basic in design but the famous "Jimmy" was the mainstay of the Allied Forces in World War II.

Specifications

Country: USA	
Year manufactured from: 1941	
Engine: six cylinder overhead valve gas and diesel	
Transmission: five-speed overdrive with two-speed transfer case	
Payload: variable	
Applications: military	
Special features: available with hard or soft cabs	

Below: The amphibious variant of the CCKW, designated DUKW, would traverse land and water equally and could cope with 50 fully equipped soldiers. The vehicles were nicknamed "Ducks."

INTERNATIONAL
✹ 1947 USA

INTERNATIONAL KB

In 1947 International continued its K series of trucks with the introduction of the KB. The new KB had a wide grille, which extended out on the front fenders.

Left: *International's KB series of trucks had a full range of sizes, including this pickup truck. Despite their small size, they were used for a wide range of hauling tasks. Before long, trucks of a similar design were surfacing in other parts of the world.*

The KB series didn't enjoy a particularly long production span, only being built between 1947 and 1949. During this time, production numbers were quite high, however. For instance about 64,000 KB-5s alone were constructed during this period. This was largely attributable to the postwar demand for trucks.

Panel bodies
The smaller models had panel bodies and could be used to haul modest loads. Wooden boxes could be found on the back of each of the models allowing for freight haulage. These trucks were commonly equipped with dump bodies. Tractor versions were also available for hauling semitrailers.

It was a stylish-looking truck with a sleek front-end and large round headlights. A long conventional-style hood provided the truck with a big-truck look and feel. It also carried the relatively new International logo featuring a red "I" over a black "H." Today, the KB series of trucks are popular choices for truck restorers. The largest of the KB series, the KB-8 had an International 360ci (5.9-liter), 126hp (93.9kw) Red Diamond engine under its hood.

Typical specs on the KB-1 included a heavy-duty clutch, rear heavy-duty springs, West Coast mirrors, and split-rim wheels with eight-ply tires. The popularity of the KB series of trucks was noticed overseas as well as in North America.

Specifications
Country: USA

Year manufactured from: 1947

Engine: up to an International 360ci (5.9- liter), 126hp (193.9kw) Red Diamond

Transmission: five-speed to bevel

Payload: 1 ton (1.016 tonne)

Applications: local pickup and delivery.

Special features: this series only enjoyed two years of production, yet was a highly popular truck during that postwar era.

FREIGHTLINER
1947   USA

FREIGHTLINER MODEL 800 "BUBBLENOSE"

Freightliner introduced its all-aluminum "Bubblenose" Model 800 cab-over-engine in 1947. The company was prospering in the postwar years and it was aggressively pursuing the use of aluminum in its truck parts.

Specifications

Country: USA

Year manufactured from: 1947

Engine: Cummins diesel

Transmission: nine-speeds to bevel

Payload: not available

Applications: long-distance, on-highway

Special features: one of the first mainstream trucks to fully utilize aluminum in an effort to minimize weight and maximize payloads.

Above: *Freightliner's Bubblenose may have looked a bit unusual, but its aluminum composition allowed carriers to increase payload by about 0.98 ton (1 tonne).*

Aluminum alloys were being widely used in Freightliner's cabs, axle housings, brake drums, cross members, wheels, radiators, and even frame rails. The company was adamant about developing a lightweight vehicle that didn't compromise strength or safety. By doing so, Freightliner trucks were able to haul 0.98 ton (1 tonne) more payload than most other trucks on the market.

The company had plenty of incentive to maximize payload because the first Freightliners were built by and for Consolidated Freightways. Since Freightliner's birth it had been providing Consolidated

Freightways with reliable transportation. However, engineers had now built a truck that was deemed ready to compete on the open market. The very first sale, to Vince Graziano, a produce hauler based in Portland, Oregon, came in 1948. He chose the Model 800 all-aluminum Bubblenose and he was so impressed by the truck that he ordered five more shortly thereafter.

In 1949 Freightliner offered a sleeper-cab version of its trucks. Later, in 1951 the company put White Motor Company in charge of sales, service, and distribution of Freightliners.

VOLVO
1953   Sweden

VOLVO VIKING L38

In the early 1950s Volvo unveiled what would become one of its most famous trucks ever—the Viking. It seemed a fitting name for the model since both Volvo itself and the ancient Vikings originated in Scandinavia.

The Viking was based on Volvo's L24 Roundnose truck. When first introduced, the Viking featured only a new hood and fenders. However, the manufacturer continued to enhance the Viking throughout the 1950s and into the early 1960s. Volvo continuously updated not only the engine strength of the Viking but also its chassis. Power steering was another feature that wasn't available on the earliest models.

International appeal

The Viking gained worldwide appeal due largely to its reliability, but it was not an overly powerful truck. In the 1950s, enormously powerful engines weren't required for road transportation in most of Europe since heavy loads were not yet the norm. The Viking was powered by a modest nominal 424.9ci (7-liter) engine, which was known for its dependability, if not its power. The original Viking engine had an output of just 100hp (74.5kw).

Throughout the 1950s, the engine received power upgrades to keep up with trends in the road transportation industry. In 1954, a genuine 424.9ci (7-liter) engine was introduced (the initial one was actually just over 364.2ci [6 liters]) along with wider fenders resembling the ones that could be found on Volvo's L39 Titan—the Viking's bigger, more powerful cousin.

The majority of Vikings manufactured were two-axle versions, however a three-axle variant was available as well. Production of the Viking ended in 1965 when it was replaced by the similar-looking N86.

Above: *The Viking was one of Volvo's most famous trucks ever.*
Above, top: *The Viking utilized a diesel engine that was known for its reliability.*

Specifications

Country: Sweden

Year manufactured from: 1953

Engine: Volvo 424.9ci (7 liter) up to 100hp (74.5kw).

Transmission: not available

Payload: not available

Applications: long-distance, on-highway, logging, off-highway

Special features: the Viking established itself as one of Volvo's most famous trucks to ever take the highway.

BEDFORD
1950s   UK

BEDFORD

After the war Bedford resumed production of its trucks using the K, M, and O models introduced in 1939 as its base. However, it wasn't long before the company replaced those trucks with more current offerings.

Above: *This S type Bedford was dubbed "The Big Bedford."*

Specifications

Country: UK

Year manufactured from: 1950s

Engine: full range of Bedford gasoline engines

Transmission: not available

Payload: 6.8 tons (7 tonnes)

Applications: long-distance, on-highway, military, local pickup and delivery.

Special features: Bedford produced full range of commercial vehicles following World War II.

The S type was known as "The Big Bedford" and it vaulted the manufacturer into the 7-ton (7-tonne) class. The truck also featured a new forward-control design. The S type was powered by a 300ci (4.9-liter) gasoline engine. It was replaced by the low-cab forward-control TK in 1960. Later is was offered with Leyland and Perkins diesels.

R type embraced by the military

The four-wheel drive R type derivative was designed in 1950 and was embraced by the military, where it served as its standard 3.9-ton (4-tonne) truck until being replaced by the MK and MJ types, and then hit the civilian market in 1953. Meanwhile, Bedford had produced the CA van, which went on to become one of its bestsellers.

In 1953 Bedford continued its aggressive product launch with the introduction of the A type, which was followed by the D and J types. These models were built well into the 1970s, with the exception of the A type, which was terminated in 1957.

The J type (or the TJ) was launched in 1958—the same year Bedford produced its millionth truck. It featured a single-piece windshield and 16in (40.6cm) road wheels providing a low body platform height on models up to 3.9 tons (4 tonnes). The TJ had a bonneted cab.

PETERBILT
1950 USA

PETERBILT 280/350

Peterbilt founder T.A. Peterman passed away in 1945 and it was a tragedy that he never lived to see one of the most innovative of the truck company's products—the Model 280/350 "Bubblenose."

This truck was developed in response to a growing Interstate highway network, which was making long-distance freight haulage by truck more practical than ever. Because not all American truckers were fond of the cab-over-engine appearance, the company also released the 281/351

conventional-styled trucks. As a result, Peterbilt had its bases covered when it came to the on-highway market.

The Bubblenose
Things were looking good for Peterbilt in 1950. The company had reached sales of

Above: The Pete 350 "Bubblenose" was a cross between a conventional and cab-over design. Most American truckers preferred a conventional truck design, but this style incorporated the best of both worlds.

$7 million and the trucking industry was becoming increasingly enamored with the truck. Still, in the rapidly changing transportation industry no company could relax. They had to continue exploring new technologies and treading new territory. Thus, the 280/350 "Bubblenose" was born.

The 280/350 model was referred to as the "Bubblenose" because it did not have a flat front like other cab-over-engines. Instead, the engine protruded slightly from the front of the cab, giving the truck what looked like a small, rounded nose. However, that nose was far shorter than the traditional conventional-style hoods of the day and the truck was classified as a cab-over-engine. Some truckers speculated the Bubblenose resulted from a shortening of the 1949 Model 360, which had a short nose that resembled a half-hood conventional.

COEs gain acceptance

The Bubblenose's cab was perched quite high compared to other models on the road at the time. The engine could be accessed by tilting the cab, but this wasn't easy to accomplish according to some truckers. They often chose to access the engine and other components by swinging the front fenders out of the way.

Two years of road testing went into the 280/350 before it was mass produced for sale to the public. The Bubblenose was a popular truck because it adhered to length restrictions being imposed in some states, especially in the eastern USA.

The Bubblenose was replaced by the 352 in 1955. The 352 was a redesigned cab-over featuring a slightly-curved four-piece windshield and it remained in Pete's product line until 1982 when the Model 362 superseded it. The 362 would have a more modern one- or two-piece flat windshield.

The 281 and 351 conventionals

Introduced in 1954, the 281 and 351 conventional models gave customers an alternative to the Bubblenose. These trucks were well liked by drivers and owners and remained in production for 11 years. They were among the first to be adorned with Peterbilt's signature red oval logo. Ironically, cab-over-engine versions of these models were introduced in late 1955.

Specifications

Country:	USA
Year manufactured from:	1950
Engine:	Cummins or GM
Transmission:	10-speed
Payload:	not available
Applications:	long-distance, on-highway
Special features:	these trucks helped pioneer the Drom-Box, which were cargo boxes attached to the back of the tractor.

Left: *The 351 was the all-American classic "conventional" tandem drive tractor, seen here with a typical sleeper compartment mounted behind the cab.*

DIAMOND T
⚒ **1950s USA**

DIAMOND T 950-951

Diamond T had made a name for itself during the war by producing what were widely thought to be the best-looking trucks in which to do battle. However, the postwar years would not be so kind to the company.

One postwar innovation was the development of a "comfort cab," which was built in conjunction with International Harvester. The 1950 cab featured a number of enhancements, such as detachable fenders and a hood that allowed outside air to pass into the engine compartment to provide better cooling and improved fuel economy. The cab also featured a four-point "diamond" mounting of the cab, sheet metal, and radiator, and had a curved windshield and concave instrument panel.

To prove how well the cab was constructed, the company subjected it to hours of severe twisting at the Chicago Auto Show that year, but no structural damage took place.

Diamond T 950-951 introduced
That same year, Diamond T introduced its 950 and 951 series of trucks, which were built at the company's Chicago factory. The 950 was built with Western truckers in mind, because they tended to demand more horsepower and larger radiators to provide adequate cooling for the larger engines. The 950 and 951 Diamond Ts were so big that, although they were a conventional design,

Above: The Diamond T 921-C tilt cab trucks of the mid-1950s could gross up to 38 tons (34.5 tonnes) and had a choice of Cummins diesels.

the driver was often perched as high as he would be in a cab-over truck.

Diesel takes over

The first of these trucks to hit the streets were equipped with gasoline engines. However, those soon gave way to the more efficient diesel-powered engines. In 1953 these trucks were paired with the tilt-cab.

In the 1950s Diamond T was focusing exclusively on the heavy-duty truck market and was only building trucks with 3 tons capacity or greater. The 950 and 951 were the largest offerings and were typically powered by a 300hp (223.7kw) Cummins diesel engine or a 280hp (208.7kw) Buda diesel.

Diamond T also built a handful of 950 RS trucks, which may well be the largest Class 8 trucks ever built for on-highway applications. It has been reported that fewer than 80 of these trucks were ever built. They were powered by Cummins diesel engines.

Diamond T honoured

In 1953 Diamond T's tilt-cab cab-over-engine truck was presented with the prestigious National Design Award for an industrial project. It was the first time any truck design had won this coveted prize. The technology which earned Diamond T the award was a

counterbalance system, which no longer made it necessary for a power unit to tilt the model 723C cab. This development was adopted by other truckmakers in years to come.

The last preacquisition Diamond Ts

While the trucking industry was awash with rumors regarding the impending acquisition of Diamond T, the company continued releasing new models. During the 1950s the company built 6x6 trucks for the military, which were powered by 224hp (167kw) Continental R6602 engines. The trucks featured automatic six-wheel drive and power steering.

The year before Diamond T was acquired by White Motor Company, it introduced the Model 831 which was driven by a 239hp (178.2kw) Hall-Scott 590 engine. This engine could burn liquid petroleum gas, which boosted its power to 256hp (190.8kw). A tilt-cab model 911C diesel was also offered before Diamond T was taken over.

Diamond T was experiencing trouble by the late 1950s. Its competitor Reo was also struggling to compete with the big players such as International, GM, and White. White Motor Company stepped in and purchased both companies in 1958 and consolidated the two brands.

Left: The tilt-cab design of the Diamond T won it the coveted National Design Award in 1953. It marked the first time a truck design had ever received the award.

Specifications

Country: USA

Year manufactured from: 1950s

Engine: 300hp (223.7kw) Cummins diesel engine or a 280hp (208.7kw) Buda diesel

Transmission: 10-speeds to bevel

Payload: not available

Applications: long-distance, on-highway, construction, off-highway

Special features: Diamond T gained fame during World War II and was known as the "best looking trucks to do war."

Below: The tilt cab fitted to Diamond T medium-weight trucks from the early 1950s had a modern appearance and was imitated by other manufacturers in subsequent years.

MACK
1953   USA

MACK G, H AND B SERIES

The 1950s were busy years for Mack, which introduced a number of advancements to its product line. The G, H, and B series trucks were among the most significant developments from the company.

In 1953 Mack introduced its new Thermodyne open chamber, direct–injection diesel engine, which set a new standard in performance and fuel efficiency. Mack's decision to make its own engines available on its trucks was seen as a bold move at the time. Other engines, including those produced by Cummins, could also be specified.

H series

The H series was introduced in 1953 and was dubbed the "Cherry Picker" because of its extremely high cab (8ft 10in [2.7m]). This

Above: *Nicknamed the "cherry picker," this truck featured an elevated driver's seat. The short BBC measurement allowed it to haul 35-ft (10.6-m) trailers.*

truck had a very short BBC, which allowed it to haul 35-ft (10.6-m) trailers. At the time the maximum overall legal length limit in many regions was 45ft (13.7m), making this a practical configuration.

They were typically powered by Mack's ENDT 673 Thermodyne, which produced up to 211hp (157.3kw) at 2,100rpm. A Quadruplex 18-speed, two-stick gearbox was another common spec. The Cherry Pickers were replaced by Mack's popular Ultra-Liner.

B series

The B series, also introduced in 1953, became one of Mack's most successful products to hit the highway. It was an easily identifiable truck thanks to its stylish, rounded appearance. The cab resembled that of a 1940s-style pickup truck rather than the big, boxy highway tractor cabs typical of this era.

More than 127,000 of these trucks were sold before production was discontinued in 1966 in favor of the R series. This line of trucks was known for its longevity and many of them are still in active service.

G series

Mack began production of the G series in 1959 and produced a total of 2,181 units by 1962. The truck featured an all-aluminum cab to reduce its weight and to allow for the haulage of heavier loads.

Specifications

Country: USA	
Year manufactured from: 1953	
Engine: Thermodyne open chamber, direct-injection diesel or Cummins	
Transmission: Quadruplex 18-speed, two stick	

Payload: not available	
Applications: long-distance, on-highway, severe-service	
Special features: H series "cherry picker" provided high sitting position for improved view of the road.	

Left: The stylish, rounded appearance of Mack's B series made it an instant hit with North American customers. The truck was a refreshing change from the "boxy" truck designs that dominated the highway at the time.

Below: The G series featured an aluminum cab, which made it possible to haul heavier loads. It was especially popular in the West Coast region of North America.

DAIMLER-BENZ
1955 Germany

DAIMLER-BENZ LP SERIES

Daimler-Benz introduced its LP series of cab-over-engine trucks in 1955 when the LP 315 7.7-ton (7-tonne) truck took to the roads. The "P" stood for "Pullman" in reference to the comfort of a Pullman car's cab.

The new trucks lacked the classic fenders and cab shape that previous generation of L series trucks were known for, and instead it had a rounded, comfortable cab design with an interior likened to that of a luxury car.

The dawn of the cab-over-engine

Prior to the introduction of the LP series, most of Daimler-Benz's trucks were hooded. COE trucks, however, were beginning to find their place in the market. The LP 315 was joined in 1958 by the LP 333 twin-steer six-wheel truck which had a 15.7-ton (16-tonne) gross vehicle weight or 31.5-tons (32-tonne) gross train weight. It was the first year

the German government had given the green light to such heavy loads.

The LPS333 is added

An LPS333 tractor was also introduced to the market and it was also rated at 31.5 tons (32 tonnes) gross combination weight. This truck's second steering axle was mid-mounted 5ft 3in (1.6m) ahead of the drive axle. Each of the LP trucks featured a full-width cab and a split windshield. However the LP 321, LP 322 and LP 337 would later be available with a smaller cab and single windshield. These later additions to the LP family were offered with payloads of 5.9 to 6.8 tons (6 to 7 tonnes).

Above: The LP series of Mercedes-Benz trucks had a cab that was intended to reflect the interior of a luxury car. To reiterate this point, the "P" in LP stood for "Pullman," a popular luxury car of that era.

Easier to understand design codes

By 1963 Daimler-Benz's cab-over-engines had undergone many changes. The LP 1620 was introduced with a gross weight of 15.7 tons (16 tonnes) and a 200hp (149kw) engine. The model names, which were obscure in the 1950s to say the least, were now easier to understand. The LP 1620, for example, referred to its gross weight and the engine horsepower.

Customers were impressed with the cab's simple, cubic design. Extended versions of most models were released with the option of a sleeper compartment for long-distance hauls. The new generation of LP trucks were generally driven by Daimler-Benz's proven six-cylinder in-line engines featuring an efficient direct-injection system and power ratings in the 210hp (156.5kw) range. It wasn't long before three-axle trucks were added to the product line.

Lightweight LPs

A new lightweight series of LP trucks was also introduced consisting of trucks with weights starting at 5.9 tons (6 tonnes) (LP 608). These cab-over-engines eventually replaced the short-nose trucks Daimler-Benz had been producing. This line of lightweight COEs was designed to look much like its bigger cousins with an angular cab,

rectangular grille, and attractive glazing. The light LP cabs were firmly mounted to the frame and were not tiltable.

More powerful engines demanded

In the mid-1960s Daimler-Benz launched the LPS 2020 three-axle rear-steer tractor unit, which was engineered to capitalize on an increase in allowable weights from 31.4 tons to 37.4 tons (32 tonnes to 38 tonnes). Because of the heavier loads anticipated as a result of the regulatory change, more powerful engines were required.

Daimler-Benz developed a new series of engines to meet these new demands and offered them in V6, V8, V10, and V12 sizes. Their power capabilities ranged from 192hp to 400hp (143.1kw to 298.2kw).

Some of the first trucks to be matched with engines from the new family were the LP and LPS 1632, 2032, and 2232 models. These trucks were identifiable because of their deep front wheel arches. The first of the new engines to hit the road was the OM403 which was a 976ci (16-liter) V10.

As a result of all these new vehicle introductions, Daimler-Benz had developed a broader product line than any other commercial manufacturer of the day. The company was a player in nearly all significant sectors of the trucking industry.

Specifications

Country: Germany

Year manufactured from: 1955

Engine: Daimler-Benz six-cylinder in-line engines

Transmission: four-speeds to bevel

Payload: not available

Applications: long-distance, on-highway, local pickup and delivery.

Special features: LP line of trucks catered to virtually every application and GVW range.

Below: *With the German government allowing heavier loads than ever, the LP was put to work delivering a range of heavy freight.*

DAF
1957   Netherlands

DAF 2000 SERIES

DAF decided to plunge into the international transportation sector in 1957 with the introduction of its 2000 series. It was a short-lived experiment, however, with the line being discontinued just two years later.

It was a unique truck, with a 9.8-ton (10-tonne) capacity rear axle—the only truck to offer this at the time. The cab was based on the A1300/1600/1800 series cab. More room was added at the front, however, to provide more cooling power.

Normal control vehicle
At about the same time the 2000 series was made available, DAF also released a normal control vehicle for specific market segments. This was known as the 12 and 15 series. In 1958, DAF began the in-house production of axles and this resulted in the need for a completely new factory. The new facility was built in Oevel, near Westerlo in Belgium. It remains in use for the production of axles today.

Above: *The 2000 model of 1957 was DAF's first truck designed for long-distance international haulage. Just five years after its launch it was superseded by the much improved 2600 model.*

The Eurotrailer unveiled

DAF continued adding new products to complement the 2000 series. One new addition to the product line was the Eurotrailer, introduced in 1962. This was a lightweight semitrailer with an integral aluminum body. DAF also surprised many during the same year by adding the 2600 truck to its lineup.

The DAF 2600 had a compact design that enabled increased payload and longer load lengths. The truck was able to accommodate a sleeper for long-distance haulage. It was quickly dubbed "The Mother of International Road Transportation."

DAF 2600 added

The 2600 launched DAF into the realms of the most respected long-distance truck manufacturers because of its increased driver comfort. It also helped DAF attain increased market share and sales and in 1964 the company produced its 50,000th truck chassis. The following year, after leading his company to success, DAF founder Hub van Doorne retired. During his reign, the company had acquired more than 100 patents.

In 1973 DAF replaced the illustrious 2600 with the 2800, which featured a cab that was 7.8in (20cm) wider. The sleeper cab could fit two full-size beds and the truck was powered by a 704ci (11.6 liter) DAF engine.

Below: Day and sleeper versions of the old DAF cab were available. The day cab shown here is on a 4x4 model for on- or off-road construction work.

Specifications

Country: Netherlands

Year manufactured from: 1957

Engine: not available

Transmission: six-speeds to bevel

Payload: not available

Applications: long-distance, international, on-highway

Special features: this truck was ultimately unable to make an impression in the long-distance international transportation segment.

GMC
1960 USA

THE NEW GMCS

In 1960 GMC completely redesigned its popular line of light-duty trucks. While light-duty in size and category, these trucks were routinely put to use hauling freight or working on North American farms.

Above: *The GMC L5000 tilt-cab model had a 180 bhp V6 gasoline engine. The heaviest L-range models had the option of a GM V-71 two-stroke diesel engine.*

Left: *The newly designed aluminum tilt-cab cruiser was nicknamed the "Crackerbox."*

The new design was radically different than its predecessor in both appearance and functionality. The new-look GMC featured a new front and rear suspension for an improved ride, and also boasted more power. They were equipped with a standard V6 engine as of 1960.

Heavy-duty cousins

While the American public was raving about the new-look light-duty GMCs, its larger cousins were also being put to work in numerous applications. The L-model was a 72in (1.8m) steel tilt-cab truck powered by a choice of engines ranging from a GMC V6 to a V12. The truck didn't change much from year to year and was discontinued in the late 1970s. The cab-over-engine trucks were commonly customized as fire trucks.

Crackerbox

At the same time, GMC was also introducing a new aluminum tilt-cab cruiser, which was nicknamed the Crackerbox. It was introduced in 1959 and sold until 1968 when it was replaced with the Astro.

The lightweight Crackerbox boasted an extra 1,824lbs (827.2kg) of payload compared to other similar trucks and measured only 48in (1.2m) from bumper to the back of cab (BBC). This short BBC also made it ideal for maneuvering in tight places.

The Crackerbox was renamed the F-model in 1960 and was available with diesel engines or GMC's own gasoline-powered engines. The truck was still known for its light weight and high payloads, however, and a sleeper was available. It measured only 22in (56cm) deep behind the driver.

Specifications

Country: USA
Year manufactured from: 1960
Engine: GMC V6-V12
Transmission: 10-speeds to bevel
Payload: not available
Applications: local pickup and delivery, long-distance, on-highway, fire
Special features: radically new design made these trucks stand out.

KENWORTH W900/K100

Two legendary Kenworth trucks were introduced in 1961—the W900 conventional and the K100 cab-over-engine. The K100 was designed to maximize cargo within state truck-length restrictions.

Above: *Kenworth's W900 (seen here on the left) made famous the long, square hood that is still popular today among North American owner-operators.*

Specifications

Country: USA

Year manufactured from: 1961

Engine: Cummins or Caterpillar six cylinder diesels

Transmission: 10-speeds to bevel

Payload: not available

Applications: long-distance, on-highway, vocational, off-highway, oilfields

Special features: tilt hood replaces the previously common butterfly-style hood.

The Kenworth W900 featured a classic look that was still popular among North American truckers, with a long hood and distinctive cathedral grille.

It found itself being thrust into all sorts of applications from rugged off-highway work to long-distance general-freight haulage. The truck could be customized for a variety of tasks, making it a diverse vehicle, and also earned a reputation for being strong and reliable.

The W900 was also designed with driver comfort in mind, which won it fans among the over-the-road crowd. The most common engine on the original W900 was a 300hp (223.7kw) Cummins turbocharged six-cylinder NTC-300. In 1982 a modified W900B was introduced.

The W900 gained plenty of attention when one was called on to deliver a high-resolution spectrometer magnet, 36,000 times stronger than the Earth's magnetic field. The load was 140ft (42.7m) long and weighed 105.3 tons (107 tonnes), but this customized W900, with a 450hp (335.6kw) Caterpillar engine and a Spicer 24-speed transmission, was able to transport the unusual shipment all the way from Illinois to Palo Alto, in California.

K100

The K100 was an important addition to Kenworth's fleet as a result of length limitations in eastern states. Operators who insisted on running a long-nose conventional truck in those regions would be forced to sacrifice payload, whereas the shorter K100 allowed fleets to maximize their carrying capacity. Of course the aerodynamics left something to be desired and in 1984 Kenworth introduced the K100E cab-over-engine, which improved air flow.

THAMES TRADER
1962   UK

THAMES TRADER

The British Ford division launched a new truck in 1958 known as the Ford Thames Trader. With a very unusual hood, this truck remained in production until 1965, when it was replaced by the D series.

Specifications

Country: UK

Year manufactured from: 1962

Engine: six cylinder gasoline or diesel engine

Transmission: five-speeds to bevel

Payload: semitrailer GCW up to 15 tons

Applications: stake body, parcel-delivery truck, dropside platform, dump, tractor unit

Special features: very distinctive semi-forward control cab

The first British Ford truck was sold under the Fordson name. When the production facilities moved from Manchester to the banks of the Thames River, the name "Fordson Thames" was adopted to give the trucks a distinct identity. The Thames name ran from 1957 to 1965. The Thames Trader was a modern semiforward-control truck that superseded the ET series. The range catered for loads from 1½ tons (1.52 tonnes) to 7 tons (7.11 tonnes), the latter being the highest payload Ford could offer on a four-wheeler rigid truck. The model number referred to the payload. So, the Thames Trader 15 was the light 1½-ton truck, the Model 20 was the 2-tonner, the Model 30 was the 3-tonner, the Model 40 was the 4-tonner, and the bigger Model 70 was the 7-tonner. In addition, some short-wheelbase tractors were built for hauling semitrailers. Two gasoline engines, and their diesel derivatives, were offered. The four-cylinder version was a 220ci (3.6-liter) gasoline engine, born in 1953 and produced as a diesel variant a year later. This engine was designed for the trucks up to 3 tons (3.05 tonnes). Above this weight, the other engine was a gasoline or diesel six-cylinder 330ci (5.41-liter) powerplant. With a total of 121,853 semiforward trucks built (along with 19,000 normal control cab trucks), the Thames Trader was a great success. Some of the trucks were exported or manufactured in Spain by the Ebro company or produced in Turkey by the Otosan company.

Above: *The Thames Trader was sometimes built as a tractor unit with a small wheelbase (9ft/2.74m), but the rigid trucks were more popular.*

MACK
1965   USA

MACK R SERIES

Mack's R series of vocational trucks introduced in 1965 earned its place in trucking history over the course of nearly four decades. The R series became the world's number one mixer and dump truck.

Above: *Mack lived up to its tough Bulldog reputation with the legendary R series.*

Right: *The Mack R series is a legendary work truck capable of severe-duty applications. It became a bestseller, with more than 360,000 units sold before its retirement in 2003.*

Specifications

Country: USA

Year manufactured from: 1965

Engine: Mack Maxidyne

Transmission: 10-speeds to bevel

Payload: not available

Applications: mixer, dump, construction, off-highway

Special features: legendary dependability and longevity made this one of the best-selling Class 8 trucks of all time.

The R series itself had big shoes to fill when first introduced as a replacement for the popular B series. However, it was a proven winner, especially when paired with Mack's new Maxidyne constant-horsepower diesel engine and the Maxitorque transmission. The Maxidyne was in fact the first high-torque rise constant-horsepower diesel engine to hit the trucking industry.

The R series trucks were immediately recognizable because of their distinctive square front-end. Some of the R series' selling points were a weight-saving design, bolted construction, a tilt-hood, and a full range of components for customers to choose from.

The staggering number of R series trucks sold in North America made it the most popular Class 8 vocational vehicle in trucking history. Mack R series customers were fiercely loyal, largely because of the model's dependability and longevity. When the RD was terminated in 2003, it was estimated that more than 200,000 of the R series trucks built over the past 38 years were still in operation.

RB and DM

While production of the RD was halted in 2003 in favor of the Granite, two other models using the R series cab continued to be built. The RB (axle back) and DM (offset cab) remained in production since the Granite was not yet available in those configurations. However, the majority of R series trucks ceased production in 1989.

PETERBILT
1967   USA

PETERBILT 359

In 1967 Peterbilt introduced the 359—a truck that would develop a loyal following of truck enthusiasts and is to this day a fixture at most North American truck shows.

Many engine choices available

You could argue it was the exterior that won the Pete 359 a devoted following. The truck featured a wide, long hood and wide grille that was an instant hit with truckers. It was only available with a tilt hood, unlike previous Petes, which featured a butterfly-style hood that was still the hood of choice among many drivers. The Peterbilt 359 really turned heads and was a big success.

Rapid expansion

Still, owner-operators who took a great deal of pride in the appearance of their rigs embraced the new truck and by 1969 Peterbilt had to construct a new factory in Madison, Tennessee, to keep up with the demand. The company had built 21,000 trucks during the 1960s, which was four times the number produced during the previous decade.

Many engine choices available

Peterbilt offered engines from manufacturers such as Caterpillar, Continental, Cummins, and Detroit Diesel. A range of engines, including V6s, V8s, straight-sixes, straight-eights, and V12s, were available under the typically large Peterbilt hoods through the 1960s.

The most common engine specification was the Cummins NH 220 diesel, which was typically paired with a Spicer 12-speed transmission. Typical axles during this era at Peterbilt were Timken full-floating hypoid or double reduction, and gross vehicle weights were up to 84,000lb (38,095kg). Gross combination weights were a staggering 250,000lb (113,376.6kg) at the time.

The Peterbilt 359 was incredibly popular until being overshadowed by the 379, which was introduced in 1977.

Above: *The Peterbilt 359 established itself as a favorite among North American owner-operators. Drivers found its long hood, wide chrome grille, and spacious interior appealing.*

Specifications

Country: USA

Year manufactured from: 1967

Engine: full range from Caterpillar, Continental, Cummins, and Detroit Diesel

Transmission: nine, 12 or 15-speeds to bevel

Payload: GVWs up to 84,000lb (38,095kg)

Applications: long-distance, on-highway

Special features: first Peterbilt to feature a tilt hood.

FORD
✖ 1970 USA

FORD L AND W SERIES

By 1970 Ford had introduced the new L (or Louisville) range of trucks to replace the normal-control T range. At the same time, Ford brought a new heavy-duty tilt-cab model known as the W series to the market.

Right: Ford's highly successful Louisville or L-line trucks announced in 1970 carried on in production until the 1990s. They sold well, not only in North America, but in many overseas markets.

Specifications

Country: USA

Year manufactured from: 1970

Engine: Cummins, Detroit Diesel, Caterpillar up to 270hp (201.3kw)

Transmission: not available

Payload: not available

Applications: long-distance, on-highway, local pickup and delivery

Special features: these trucks represented Ford's last efforts in the Class 8 market

These trucks were built at what was the world's largest truck factory at the time capable of producing 336 trucks a day.

Louisville range embraced

The W series trucks featured a 52in (1.32m) BBC and had a square look to the cab. There was also an 82in (2.08m) BBC sleeper-equipped W series truck available. Four different Cummins engines could be matched with these trucks offering a total of 13 different power ratings. Detroit Diesel and Caterpillar engines were also options and most delivered between 250 and 270hp (186.4 and 201.3kw). The L range was

extremely successful and was in production for more than 20 years. The L-9000 and LT-9000 in particular were embraced by the trucking industry and many considered these trucks to be the manufacturer's first real successful foray into the conventional diesel haul market.

The W series, on the other hand, received an overhaul in 1975 at which time it was given a new grille that looked much like the one found on the more popular L series. The W series was replaced in the late 1970s by the all-aluminum CL-9000.

In 1997 Ford sold its heavy-duty truck operations to Freightliner. ·

VOLVO

1977 Sweden

VOLVO F10 AND F12

Volvo made history when it introduced its F10 and F12 trucks in 1977. The Swedish manufacturer revolutionized the trucking industry with these two models, which set a new standard for ergonomics and safety.

Above: *The F12 was capable of extremely demanding duties, such as hauling logs through the hilly Scandinavian terrain.*

To help design one of the safest commercial trucks on the road, Volvo established a special group of people who would investigate all truck accidents in Sweden and determine what went wrong. The ultimate goal was to design safer trucks and learn from the mistakes of the past. At the same time, special attention was being given to ergonomics. A more conveniently designed and comfortable truck is ultimately a safer truck. The solutions that were reached by designers and the safety team were not only implemented in the F10 and F12, but in every other Volvo truck developed since then.

Volvo opted to use chassis and driveline components that had been in use since 1973 on the N line of trucks to ensure some commonality between the models. These components had already proven themselves in a wide range of applications and the philosophy of "If it ain't broke, don't fix it" was followed when it came to these parts.

Instead, Volvo engineers directed their attention to improving safety through other modifications to the vehicle. One new development was fitting the cab to the chassis with a spiral suspension to improve driver comfort and ride. This simple change was effective in reducing the back pain suffered by many long-haul truckers.

Adjustable steering wheel

The steering wheel was made adjustable so the driver could set it at his or her preferred location and angle. In addition, the windshield size was increased so drivers had better visibility, reducing the risk of an accident. More enhancements for convenience were also introduced into the F10 and F12 models, including a luggage compartment, which was accessible from the exterior, but locked from the inside to prevent theft. This was a nice touch for long-distance truckers—the main target market for these trucks.

Injury prevention a priority

Despite its best efforts, Volvo realized accidents could not be completely eliminated. The company worked hard to make the interior of the truck as safe as possible so drivers had a better chance of escaping injury in the event of an accident.

Padding was added to the inside of the cab and virtually every sharp edge was eliminated. And, naturally, the cab was tested to the stringent Swedish cab test standards, which were the most demanding in the world.

Driver health was also a motivation for the new integrated air-conditioning system. In Europe, previous air-conditioning systems consisted of air being blown through a single vent, which wasn't healthy. Volvo's new integrated system alleviated this problem and so was a popular feature of the F10 and F12.

Slightly heavier

Customers were not deterred by the fact that the cab weighed more than some of the other less safety-oriented cabs on the market. For most, the trade-off in weight was worthwhile given the safety enhancements. The F10 and F12 were developed before advanced computer-aided design techniques were available. The F10 and F12 cab featured a flat roof, but the Globetrotter cab was made available in 1979 for operators craving some extra space.

Volvo continuously enhanced the F10 and F12 over the next few years and by the mid-1990s more than 200,000 of these trucks had been sold.

Inset: The F10 and F12 cabs weighed slightly more than other comparable cabs, but customers didn't mind because safety was enhanced so drastically.

Specifications

Country: Sweden

Year manufactured from: 1977

Engine: 586- and 732ci (9.6- and 12-liter) Volvo

Transmission: not available

Payload: not available

Applications: long-distance, on-highway

Special features: one of the safest cabs ever produced at the time.

Left: Volvo's F10 and F12 trucks set a new standard for safety and ergonomics. The cab was the company's safest yet, thanks in part to the formation of a Volvo Safety Team that investigated accidents and took steps to address any problem areas.

KENWORTH
1985 USA

KENWORTH T600A/T800

Kenworth introduced the T600A in 1985, a revolutionary sloped-nose conventional tractor with a front axle that was set back. The result was the comfort of a conventional and the maneuverability of a cab-over.

At first, truckers were slow to embrace the radical new design. American truckers have traditionally enjoyed the long, square, conventional-style hoods Kenworth and Peterbilt were known for. The new-look T600A took some getting used to. Money talks, however, and with diesel prices reaching new heights it wasn't long before truckers were willing to give it a shot.

Massive fuel savings

The T600A was more aerodynamic than its predecessors, which helped customers shave up to 22 percent off their fuel costs. Compared with Kenworth's W900 conventional, the T600A delivered aerodynamics that were 40 percent better. The company admitted it had originally feared the radical new styling might turn off some customers. In the end, the gamble paid off because it has earned its spot at the top of Kenworth's best-seller list.

Still basking in the success of the T600A, Kenworth launched the T800 a year later. This truck featured a set-back front axle for maximum payload and maneuverability but

Above: *The T600A and the T800 (seen here) accounted for half of Kenworth's production by the mid 1990s.*

it was designed for heavier-duty operations. It was also suitable for off-highway applications such as logging and mining. The T600 and T800 have been frequently updated since their introduction. The two models accounted for half of Kenworth's production by the mid-1990s. While engineers continue to find ways of saving even more fuel with the T600 and T800 series, unfortunately for truckers, the cost of diesel seems to be keeping up with any enhancements.

Today's T600

Kenworth insists its T600 is without equal when it comes to aerodynamics, performance, and driver comfort. It is an ideal truck for linehaul operations (movement of products between two customer locations, for example, a local warehouse and a regional distribution center) thanks to its exceptional aerodynamics, and its set-back front axle provides excellent maneuverability and weight distribution.

The truck can be customized for a range of applications including regional pickups and deliveries. Bulk haulers demanding high payload capacity can also trim it out through a variety of weight-saving options. One could say it's the truck for every job.

Drivers appreciate its quiet cab and conveniently located gauges and controls. It also provides a smooth ride because of its 64in (162.5cm) front springs, a proprietary eight-bag air suspension as well as a cab and/or sleeper suspension. To all this is added the fact that the T600 is known for its ease of maintenance and high resale values and it's no wonder the model has proved to be one of Kenworth's most successful.

Today's T600 can be matched with a wide number of engines ranging between 610 and 976ci (10 and 16 liters) and up to 600hp (447.4kw). The front axles are available in ratings between 12,000 and 14,600lb (5,454 and 6,636kg) while the rear axles are rated at 23,000lb (10,455kg) for singles and 46,000lb (20,909.6kg) for tandems. The sleepers that are available on the T600 line range from the 38in (96.5cm) AeroCab FlatTop to the more spacious 86in (2.18m) Studio AeroCab.

Left: *The T600A was an immediate hit with long-distance haulers where fuel mileage was a major concern. The sloped nose remains popular today.*

Specifications

Country: USA

Year manufactured from: 1985

Engine: full range up to 600hp (447.4kw)

Transmission: nine or 15-speeds to bevel

Payload: not available

Applications: long-distance, on-highway

Special features: sloped hood claimed to reduce fuel consumption by 22 percent.

Below: *The aerodynamic T600A was a radical departure from Kenworth's traditional long-nose conventional-styled truck. While it took some getting used to, even Kenworth loyalists couldn't argue with a 22 percent fuel savings.*

IVECO
1984 Italy

IVECO TURBOSTAR

Iveco was founded in the mid-1970s, but it struggled to produce trucks that reflected its own corporate identity. This could be partly attributed to the fact that it was comprised of various factories and companies.

Specifications

Country: Italy
Year manufactured from: 1984
Engine: Iveco 8210 842ci (13.8-liter), 330hp (246kw), or the Iveco 8280 1,049ci (17.2-liter) with 420hp (313.1kw)
Transmission: eight-speeds to bevel
Payload: not available
Applications: heavy-duty, long-distance
Special features: TurboStar was Iveco's first success in heavy-duty truck market.

However, in 1984 Iveco introduced the TurboStar, which attracted some attention in the trucking industry and helped establish the company as a real player in the commercial-vehicle industry. The TurboStar was a huge success in the heavy-duty truck sector. The truck's popularity could be attributed in large part to the cab and engine.

The cab looked similar to those produced by FIAT, but it included many enhancements including an interior height of 5ft 7in (1.7m). The cab was more comfortable than other common cabs of the day and a softer suspension system also contributed to the TurboStar's popularity because it delivered a smoother ride. Iveco referred to the truck as the first real blend of different cultures, which had been the focus of Iveco's efforts right from the start. The Iveco TurboStar became famous as the car-hauler of choice for the Ferrari Formula 1 team.

Most powerful engine available

The TurboStar could be purchased with one of two engines. They included the 8210 842ci (13.8-liter) straight-six turbo with 330hp (246kw), or the 8280 1,049ci (17.2-liter) behemoth with 420hp (313.1kw). The latter, a V8, was one of the most powerful engines available in any truck at the time making the TurboStar an ideal truck for heavy-duty haulage. It was particularly popular for long-distance and international transportation.

Above: *The Turbostar was Iveco's first real success in the heavy-duty long-distance trucking sector. An interior height of 5ft 6in (1.7 metres) made it an ideal truck for long-distance haulage.*

SCANIA 3-SERIES
⚒ **1988 Sweden**

SCANIA 3-SERIES

Scania introduced its 3-series in 1988 as a successor to the popular 2-series of heavy-duty trucks. Most of the developments incorporated into the 3-series revolved around the powertrain.

Above: *While the Scania 3-series closely resembled its 2-series predecessor, it incorporated numerous refinements to improve performance and reduce emissions.*

Right: *Scania's 3-series was highly customizable and available in a wide range of configurations. Its reliability helped win it European Truck of the Year honors in 1989.*

Specifications

Country: Sweden	
Year manufactured from: 1988	
Engine: full range	
Transmission: five or 10-speeds to bevel	
Payload: not available	
Applications: long-distance, on-highway	
Special features: winner of the European Truck of the Year award in 1989.	

However, improvements were by no means limited just to the drivetrain components. The 2-series' dashboard was replaced with a new, more ergonomic type that curved toward the driver, providing easy access to important gauges and instruments. The driver also enjoyed a smoother ride thanks to a cab with four-point suspension.

The Scania 3-series was very well received by the trucking industry and it took top honors as Truck of the Year in Europe in 1989. It was the first time an entire truck range had won the award. The Truck of the Year jury commented that the 3-series boasted: "A generally high standard of engineering, top-class driving comfort combined with a high standard of driver and passenger safety, advanced engines offering good fuel consumption, and superb reliability."

Modular design

With the development of the 3-series, Scania was forging ahead with its modular approach. The manufacturer was producing "made-to-measure" trucks for specific customers, depending on their individual needs. Customers were able to specify exactly which components they wanted on their vehicle.

MACK

1988   USA

MACK CH

Mack Trucks introduced its CH highway lineup to the North American trucking industry in 1988. The CH was an axle-forward vehicle suitable for on- and off-highway stop-and-go applications.

Left: *Mack referred to its CH series as one of the most versatile trucks on the road. It was put to the test in many applications both on- and off-highway.*

A CH day cab was included in the line, which was ideal for lightweight bulk haul, van, flatbed, and lowboy applications, the company said. At the time of its release, Mack said the CH was one of the most versatile trucks on the road because it could be customized for a wide variety of heavy-duty highway and vocational applications. A range of horsepower ratings were available, which could be paired with various transmissions to deliver optimum performance.

When designing the CH cab, engineers set out to combine the best ergonomic styling with traditional heavy-truck features. For instance, switches and gauges were placed within easy reach of the driver while the dashboard was well-lit, making it more visible. The cab was mounted on an air-ride suspension to give a smooth ride. The driver's view was enhanced by the sloped hood.

Three sleepers

Mack provided three types of sleeper box for the CH series including 48in, 56in, and 70in (1.21m, 1.42m, and 1.77m) options. Engineers utilized every inch of the cab's space by providing plenty of storage in areas such as the space under the bunk. Improved insulation within the sleeper box provided a more comfortable environment.

Specifications

Country:	USA
Year manufactured from:	1988
Engine:	Mack ASET
Transmission:	10-speeds to bevel
Payload:	not available
Applications:	heavy-duty on- and off-highway, vocational
Special features:	set-forward axle provides excellent maneuverability.

KENWORTH
✷ 1989 USA

KENWORTH W 900L

At the end of 1989, Kenworth launched the W 900L (L for "Long"), with an extended hood. It was a special variant of the great W 900, which is still manufactured after more than four decades.

Right: The Kenworth W 900L remains by far the most stylish American truck in the world, with a massive square radiator and an external stainless air filter.

Specifications

Country: USA

Year manufactured from: 1989

Engine: Caterpillar or Cummins up to 600hp (447kw)

Transmission: full range

Payload: up to 200,000 GCW, normally 80,000 GCW

Applications: long-distance, on-highway

Special features: extended hood 130in (330cm) BBC, engines up to 600 hp (447kw).

With the introduction of new big six-inline turbocharged and aftercooled engines from Cummins and Caterpillar (up to 600hp/447kw), Kenworth had to change some details of the famous W 900: an extended hood and bigger radiator were now necessary. The result was the new W 900L. The tilted fiberglass hood was so long that it was gently sloped to improve the visibility.

Classic styling

Of course, the W 900L kept the classic styling of its predecessors, with plenty of chrome, decorative stainless-steel parts, and custom upholsteries. There are now 19 interior color options and three main trim levels (Splendor, Diamond, and Diamond VIT—Very Important Truck). For comfort, the handcrafted Studio Sleeper and the Aerocab/Aerodyne Sleepers give the riders plenty of room and a much more of a just-like-home feel. In order to save weight, the sleepers and the cab are made of corrosion-proof aluminum and fiberglass materials. A modern air-suspension system provides a great smooth ride.

With a length of 130in (330cm) bumper to back of cabin (BBC), the W 900L is specially designed for long-haul applications and hill climbing and for owner-operators. It has a high resale value, and the W 900L remains the spearhead of Kenworth, even if it's not the best seller of the company since the introduction of the T 600 and the T 800.

VOLVO
✗ **1993 Sweden**

VOLVO FH SERIES

Volvo's FH series, introduced in 1993, has been a true success story for the Swedish manufacturer. The FH12 and FH16 have been heralded as among the most popular trucks ever to take to the highway.

One of the factors contributing to the FH series' success was its cutting-edge technology, which helped improve areas such as fuel efficiency. The FH12 was powered by an all-new 732ci (12-liter) D12A engine engineered by Volvo. The FH16, meanwhile, featured a revamped Volvo 976ci (16-liter) engine that was first introduced in 1987 under the hood of the F16.

The D12A was designed for use on both sides of the Atlantic. It was the first European-designed diesel truck engine to boast a high-pressure unit fuel injector and overhead camshaft along with four valves per cylinder. This combination provided better breathing for the engine, which led to higher efficiency and lower fuel consumption. This technology was previously only found in advanced passenger car engines. In addition, it helped reduce emissions, which was becoming more of an issue in the 1990s.

The D12A also featured Volvo's own engine brake, which contributed to the safety of the new engine. The Volvo Engine

Above: The FH16 looked much like its less powerful cousin, the FH12, but a 976ci (16-liter) engine provided considerably more power.

Brake was necessitated by the engine's ability to maintain higher average speeds, which caused more strain on the brakes. Volvo's Accident Commission—a team that has investigated accidents for more than 25 years—also lent its expertise to the designers to ensure the FH series was as safe as possible.

Aerodynamic cab

The FH12 and FH16 featured cabs that were designed with the driver in mind. Fuel efficiency was also a motivation for engineers, and they designed the cab to be aerodynamic and lightweight without sacrificing any of the comforts drivers expected and enjoyed. In fact, while making the cab more efficient and productive, designers also made it quieter and more comfortable. Three cab versions were introduced for the FH12 and FH16. They included a short day cab, long sleeper cab, and the Globetrotter, a long sleeper cab with interior standing room. Two years later the even larger Globetrotter XL was introduced.

More enhancements introduced

The FH became the first heavy-duty truck to be equipped with a driver's side airbag in 1995, according to Volvo. This introduction elevated the truck's passive safety to a whole new level.

In 1998 the FH vehicles received a facelift and the result was the second Truck of the Year Award for the lineup, which was presented in 2000. The FH series received its first such accolade in 1994 following its introduction. The look of the truck changed somewhat as a result of the enhancements. The front of the cab was altered to improve airflow and increase the efficiency of the headlights. Another safety feature was introduced along with the new FH series at this time—Volvo's new electronically controlled heavy-duty disk brakes.

Another enhancement introduced in the late 1990s was the new D12C engine. It had been completely retooled to provide better performance and greater fuel economy as well as extended service life and even better environmental characteristics. The new engine was developed with impending Euro 3 emissions standards in mind, which were to come into play in 2001.

Volvo halted production of the FH16 in 2001, but in 2003 it came out with a completely new 976ci (16-liter) in-line six cylinder direct-injection diesel engine with overhead camshaft, four valves per cylinder, and electronic unit fuel injectors.

Left: *Many truck enthusiasts insist Volvo's FH12 was the most successful truck to ever be built. The critics agreed, naming the FH-series Volvo the Truck of the Year in 1994 and 2000, the first time a single truck won the award twice.*

Specifications

Country: Sweden	
Year manufactured from: 1993	
Engine: Volvo D12 A or D16A	
Transmission: nine or 14-speeds to bevel	
Payload: 9.8 to 39.4 tons (10 to 40 tonnes)	
Applications: long-distance, on-highway, logging	
Special features: Volvo Engine Brake provided stopping power to reduce strain on foundation brakes.	

Left: *The FH12 could be purchased with the Globetrotter cab, which was big enough to allow a driver to stand up inside. An even larger Globetrotter XL cab was introduced soon after.*

MERCEDES-BENZ
1996 Germany

MERCEDES-BENZ ACTROS

As the successor to the popular 23-year-old Mercedes-Benz SK, the new Actros had big shoes to fill. However, the Actros' engineers endeavored to deliver improved driver comfort and better performance.

Above: *The Actros cab was designed to stringent safety standards and could be ordered with a driver's side airbag.*

Specifications

Country: Germany
Year manufactured from: 1996
Engine: V6 or V8
Transmission: MB Telligent gearbox
Payload: 25 to 28 tonnes (24.6 to 27.5 tons)
Applications: long-distance on-highway
Special features: stability control system helps prevent rollovers.

Above, left: *The Mercedes-Benz Actros incorporated new technology, such as an automated gearbox that calculated the appropriate gear based on torque and engine speed. It was a popular long-distance highway truck that was easy to drive.*

One of the most interesting developments to be implemented in the Actros was the Telligent engine system, which was constantly provided with key information so it could make the proper injection duration and timing decisions for each cylinder. The result of this precise engine control was high power output, low fuel consumption, and lower emissions.

The Actros also featured a Telligent gearshift system mounted on the side of the seat that could simply be moved up or down to change gears. The Telligent gearbox is able to calculate the appropriate gear and automatically chooses the right one based on torque and engine speed.

The driver could override the gearbox's decision, but in most cases the driver would simply depress the clutch to accept the decision and the truck would change gears accordingly. A rocker switch allows the driver to shift up or down half a gear and if the driver tries to shift into the incorrect gear the system will give a warning.

Safety first

The Actros' cab was tested to ECE R 29 standards and a driver's side airbag was optional. The optional Telligent roll control system automatically adjusted the shock absorbers based on operating conditions and load characteristics.

KENWORTH

1996 USA

KENWORTH T2000

Kenworth, traditionally known for its conventional styling, released its aerodynamic highway tractor, the T2000, in 1996. The T2000 was designed to strike a fine balance in pleasing both driver and owner.

Above: *Twenty years of aerodynamic retooling went into the design of the T2000. Lightweight components were also used to further improve the trucks' fuel mileage.*

Specifications

Country: USA

Year manufactured from: 1996

Engine: full range 607 to 976ci (10- to 16-liter), up to 600hp (447.4kw)

Transmission: nine or 15-speeds to bevel

Payload: approx 20 tons (20.3 tonnes)

Applications: long-distance on-highway, regional hauling

Special features: sloping hood provides improved aerodynamics, radically new look.

Above, right: *The T2000 featured a huge, 75in (1.9m) sleeper making it an instant hit with long-distance truckers in the North American market. While it was a departure from Kenworth's long, square hood, its improved fuel mileage won it fans among both fleets and owner-operators.*

The truck was unveiled at the International Trucking Show where it was presented in 112 and 120in (2.84 and 3.04m) BBC configurations with 75in (1.9m) AERODYNE sleepers. The cab was bonded and fastened using aerospace technologies that provided a smooth, durable, and weather-tight design.

Twenty years of aerodynamic research

The company said the T2000 was the culmination of 20 years of aerodynamic tooling by the company's engineers. Advanced composite materials, lightweight components, and improved aerodynamics combined to make the T2000 a more efficient vehicle to operate in over-the-road applications.

The hood, windshield, fairing, bumper, fenders, and cab extension were all designed with aerodynamics in mind. Load capacity was also increased thanks to the lightweight components. While setting a new standard for aerodynamics, Kenworth also said the T2000 raised the bar in terms of comfort, performance, and reliability and was designed with reducing life-cycle costs in mind.

Drivers were pleased with the T2000's intelligent use of space and ergonomic cab design, which contributed to a better lifestyle while on the road. A thermal core floor provided excellent insulating qualities.

DAF

DAF 95XF

DAF introduced the new 95XF in 1997, promising to deliver lower operating costs, improved reliability, and enhanced driver comfort. The 95XF was named the International Truck of the Year in 1998.

Below: DAF vowed the 95XF was the perfect truck for heavy and long-distance hauling. The truck's engines boasted up to 530hp (396.2kw) ensuring it could live up to its reputation as a heavy hauler.

Left: The DAF XF's Space and Super Space cabs provided plenty of living space for long-haul drivers. More than 35 cubic feet (1 cu m) of storage space was provided with no nook or cranny going to waste.

The 95-series had been around for 10 years prior to the release of the 95XF. However, the 95XF took the series to a new level, especially in terms of driver comfort.

Spacious cabs available

Several previously available cab sizes were dropped on the 95XF in favor of the larger Space and Super Space Cabs. Customers wanting the smaller cab sizes could opt for DAF's more modest 85-series vehicles. Both the Space Cab and Super Space Cab proved to be winners. They not only provided plenty of space, but were also very quiet.

Other features of the Space Cab and Super Space Cab included spacious lockers over the windshield, a central compartment that could accommodate a microwave oven, and storage underneath the lower bunk. There was also an airtight storage area accessible only from outside the vehicle, which could be used to store dirty or smelly objects. The total storage capacity of the Super Space Cab was more than 35 cubic feet (1 cubic metre).

The 95XF provided operators with more powerful engine choices, including Euro-2 and Euro-3 compliant engines ranging from 380 to 480hp (283.3 to 357.9kw). Despite the powerful engines and large cab, the 95XF delivered very good fuel mileage.

Specifications

Country: Netherlands

Year manufactured from: 1997

Engine: DAF or Cummins up to 530hp (395.2kw)

Transmission: 16-speeds to bevel

Payload: 24.6 to 68.9 tons (25 to 70 tonnes)

Applications: heavy and long-distance hauling

Special features: large cabs make it ideal truck for long-distance transportation.

SCANIA
1998 Sweden

SCANIA 4-SERIES

In 1998 Scania released its 4-series of trucks covering a range of heavy transportation requirements from local delivery to long-distance heavy haulage. The 4-series also complied with tough environmental standards.

Above, top: *Driver comfort was one of the top selling points for Scania.*

Above: *The Scania 4-series was environmentally friendly.*

The 4-series was divided into four different classes, making it easy for customers to choose the vehicle that best suited their individual needs. Each of the classes boasted a high level of driver comfort and safety and was easy to modify.

The Class L chassis was designed for long-distance haulage on regular roads. This particular truck could handle payloads with gross weights up to of 59 tons (60 tonnes). It could be equipped with engines of up to 530hp (395.2kw). The Class L chassis could be fitted with low, high, high-roof, or hooded day cabs or sleeper cabs. It was the ideal truck for international road haulage.

The Class D chassis featured low maintenance costs and good fuel mileage. The powertrain, chassis, and cab were reinforced, providing excellent reliability. It was best suited for short distances on normal roads and had a maximum gross weight of up to 43.3 tons (44 tonnes). Engines of up to 385hp (287kw) could be specified and low day cabs or sleeper cabs were both options.

A model for every road type

The C class was designed for demanding jobs over short distances, and was an excellent off-road vehicle thanks to its high ground clearance. The C class could handle gross weights of up to 147.6 tons (150 tonnes) and could be powered by engines up to 530hp (395.2kw). Often, the C class was put to work in the construction of heavy special transportation sectors. The sturdy powertrain, chassis, and cab made this a reliable vehicle.

FREIGHTLINER
1998 USA

FREIGHTLINER CENTURY CLASS S/T/ARGOSY

With the turn of the century fast approaching, Freightliner introduced its Century Class S/T in 1998. The new model featured a state-of-the-art aerodynamic design and an under-the-hood air-management system.

Specifications

Class S/T/Argosy
Country: USA
Year manufactured from: 1998
Engine: full range, Detroit Diesel, Mercedes-Benz, and Caterpillar
Transmission: nine or 12-speeds to bevel
Payload: 19.7 tons (approx 20 tonnes)
Applications: long-haul, on-highway
Special features: COE Argosy able to haul 58-ft (17.6-m) trailers, increasing load capacity.

Above: *With very few cab-over-engine trucks running American highways, Freightliner gambled with the introduction of the Argosy. It allowed operators to haul longer loads, but conventional-style trucks would remain dominant in North America.*

The Mercedes-Benz wind tunnel in Stuttgart, Germany, helped engineers reach new heights when it came to aerodynamics and fuel efficiency, and designers on both sides of the Atlantic contributed to the new model. Safety enhancements such as the introduction of driver's side air bags to the heavy-duty truck market were also achieved.

Aerodynamic hood

The Century Class featured a low, aerodynamic hood, which provided improved visibility and better fuel consumption as a result of improved air flow over the front of the truck. It was a lightweight, yet strong hood constructed of a sheet-molded compound. A larger windshield and mirrors also contributed to improved visibility from the driver's seat.

One of the more cutting-edge developments found inside the cab was a Driver Message Center, which provided information to the driver about such things as fuel economy, mileage, fluid levels, and other onboard systems. It also provided timely information about any attention or repairs the truck required.

MACK
1999 USA

MACK VISION

Mack introduced its premium highway tractor—the Vision—in 1999. It was designed to provide excellent handling and driver comfort as well as low operating costs and excellent efficiency.

Above: *The Mack Vision was a premium highway tractor with excellent aerodynamics.*

Specifications

Country: USA

Year manufactured from: 1999

Engine: Mack ASET

Transmission: 12 or 16-speeds to bevel

Payload: 19.7 tons (20 tonnes)

Applications: long-haul, on-highway, heavy bulk, dump

Special features: latest generation of engines feature EGR to reduce emissions (as of 2002).

The Vision featured an aerodynamically designed hood, grille, and cab, giving it a modern highway-tractor appearance. Drivers enjoyed the ergonomic layout of the cab, which included an electronic wraparound dashboard.

The Vision also provided a smooth ride thanks to the air-suspended cab and sleeper combination. The sleepers were available in a range of sizes including 48in (1.2m) flattop, 56in (1.4m) flattop, 60in (1.5m) mid-rise, and 70in (1.7m) mid-rise. The Vision was also available as a day cab for those operators who wanted a lightweight vehicle and didn't require the extra living space afforded by a sleeper cab.

Vision day cab

The Vision day cab featured an axle-back chassis and could be customized with a variety of axles, transmissions, and suspensions. One such suspension was the MaxAir, with 12,000lb (5442.1kg) front and 40,000lb (18,140.5kg) rear axles. For operators planning on putting their Vision to work in flatbed, dump trailer, and heavy-bulk applications, two frames were available including inside channel reinforcement.

MAN
2000 Germany

MAN TG-A

MAN introduced its Trucknology Generation A as a versatile range built in a modular fashion, which the company said would set the standards for optimum payload. The MAN TG-A won Truck of the Year in 2001.

The "Trucknology" phrase was coined by MAN executives to describe the advanced engineering and design that went into the TG-A. The truck was launched amid much fanfare in the year 2000 to an audience of more than 8,000 guests at simultaneous events across the United Kingdom.

Modification of the TG-A was still possible thanks to an assortment of wheelbase and overhang combinations available from MAN. Custom bodies could be easily modified to the requirements of a specific job.

Heavy payloads

The product range included a 6x2 chassis, which was capable of taking on jobs involving extremely heavy loads, and five different cabs were available so customers could choose the configuration best suited to their application and haulage distances. MAN referred to this option as a "space travel" program for both payload and driver. The MAN TG-A boasted a custom-fit drivetrain and a choice of four Euro 3 compliant engines. Six-cylinder powerplants were the norm, capable of up to 460hp (343kw) while yielding high torque outputs. Despite the power of these engines, they ran very quietly.

A strong, yet weight-optimized frame helped improve payload capacity on the TG-A. Drivers enjoyed a pneumatic spring system provided enhanced driving stability and a comfortable ride.

Above: *The MAN TG-A trucks, such as these 410 models were known for their high payloads, as they were comprised of lightweight components and materials.*

Specifications

Country: Germany

Year manufactured from: 2000

Engine: MAN 732 and 781ci (12 and 12.8 liter)engines

Transmission: 12 or 16-speeds to bevel

Payload: not available

Applications: long-haul, on-highway

Special features: optional aerodynamics package reduces fuel usage.

IVECO

🛠 **2002 Italy**

IVECO STRALIS RANGE

In January 2002, Iveco introduced its Stralis Range line of heavy-duty trucks. First came the Active Space model, followed shortly thereafter by the introduction of the Active Time and Active Day models.

Above: *The Iveco Stralis range included the 350 (left) and the 430 (right) heavy-duty models.*

Specifications

Country: Italy
Year manufactured from: 2002
Engine: Iveco Cursor
Transmission: automated EuroTronic 12-speeds to bevel
Payload: 27.6 tons (28 tonnes)
Applications: local delivery to long-distance international haulage
Special features: winner of the 2003 International Truck of the Year award

The Active Space was designed with the long-distance and international hauler in mind. It has plenty of cab room and a large, comfortable sleeper compartment, while the Active Time has been marketed to drivers who haul short or medium distances and don't require a large sleeper box. It does, however, include a bunk and is ideal for short trips away from home. The Active Day model is intended for regional delivery drivers who don't sleep in their truck.

2003 International Truck of the Year

The Active Space took top honors as the International Truck of the Year in 2003. The cabs of both the Active Time and Active Day were lowered 5.9in (15cm) to make it easier for drivers to enter and exit, reducing driver fatigue. The cab suspension was also modified to reduce vibration.

The major selling point for the Stralis line was its fuel consumption. Company officials boldly claimed the Active Space delivered 4 to 5 percent better fuel mileage than the competition. This was largely due to a new aerodynamic profile. Each of the Stralis Range models was also designed to reduce maintenance costs. This was achieved through the use of new engine technology.

INTERNATIONAL
2004 USA

INTERNATIONAL 9000I-SERIES

The International 9000i series of highway tractors consists of popular fleet trucks such as the aerodynamic 9200i as well as more conventional-styled trucks such as the International Eagle 9900ix.

Specifications

Country: USA

Year manufactured from: 2004

Engine: wide range of Caterpillar and Cummins engines

Transmission: full range of Fuller and Meritor transmissions

Payload: approx 20 tons (20.3 tonnes) on line haul

Applications: long-distance transportation

Special features: aerodynamics make it two to five percent more fuel efficient than previous models

The International 9200i features an aerodynamic shape that makes it between 2 and 5 percent more fuel efficient than traditional models. It has a set-back front axle to provide improved maneuverability and also offers drivers an excellent view of the highway. The truck is lightweight thanks in part to an aluminum cab—another reason for its popularity with fleets which can take advantage of this by hauling longer trailers and heavier loads. The 9200i is also popular with drivers because it boasts an abundance of storage space and plenty of room to move.

Traditional look

What separates the International Eagle 9900ix is the Eagle trim, which can be found inside and outside the cab. The Eagle 9900ix has plenty of stainless steel on the exterior, giving it a classic look as well as a full-width Texas Style front bumper.

Above: *The International Eagle became a popular long-distance truck among North American fleets. It features a lightweight, aluminum cab and an aerodynamic hood.*

RENAULT

2004 France

RENAULT MAGNUM

Renault's flagship vehicle is the popular Magnum, which can be an effective highway truck operating in most applications. The Magnum is a common sight on European highways.

Above: *The Magnum is Renault's flagship model in Europe.*

Inset: *The instantly recognizable Diamond badge has been Renault's symbol since 1925.*

Specifications

Country: France
Year manufactured from: 2004
Engine: E-Tech six cylinder engine
Transmission: not available
Payload: 2.7 tons (2.7 tonnes)
Applications: suitable for all highway applications
Special features: Multipass cab delivers "a true living space."

What makes the Magnum stand out from other highway trucks is the fact that the cab is physically removed from the driveline components. The Multipass cab sits above, and slightly separated from what the company refers to as the "technical module," which houses the engine, transmission, and other components. The result is a distinctive style and shape that make the Magnum immediately recognizable.

Other unique styling elements incorporated in the latest generation of the Magnum include a flexible spoiler with built-in foglights and trapezoid, single-piece headlights that provide excellent visibility at night.

"A true living space"

The French manufacturer refers to the Multipass cab as a "true living space" that provides drivers with an ergonomic driving position, thermal and sound insulation against outside temperatures and noise, as well as reduced warmup time for added driver comfort. The Multipass cab is designed to reflect an actual apartment, with several distinct areas including a dining room, living room, and bedroom. A swiveling passenger seat represents an armchair, complete with footrest. The latest Magnum also includes plenty of storage space so operators can enjoy more room to move within the cab. The Magnum is a popular choice among drivers because of its many comforts.

Picture Credits

All pictures supplied by Francis Dreer/Big Block
except for the following:

Index